What people are saying about …

Curious Faith

"*Curious Faith* has challenged me in the best of ways to give up my tendency to control and let Him write my story instead. If you've been holding a tight grip on your life, let Logan's words remind you that God has a beautiful plan for you—one you never could have orchestrated on your own—if you trust in Him!"

Lysa TerKeurst, *New York Times* bestselling
author and president of Proverbs 31 Ministries

"Inordinate, everyday curiosity shows you how to find the coordinates of God's everyday grace. With fresh vision and vibrant faithfulness, Logan Wolfram hands you a needed compass with these pages."

Ann Voskamp, author of the *New York Times* bestsellers *One Thousand Gifts* and *The Greatest Gift*

"I'm a pastor's kid who grew up thinking 'faith' meant leaping into the unknown. But my friend Logan Wolfram has changed all that. I now realize it means leaping into the heart of One who knows us. Into the heart of One who eclipses the moon; who holds every baby—even the ones we lose—and who calls us sons and daughters of the King. With transparency, humor, and poetry, Wolfram awakens the spirit and calls out curiosity—a longing for more of God. A must-read."

Emily T. Wierenga, founder of The Lulu
Tree and author of the memoirs *Atlas Girl* and
Making It Home (www.emilywierenga.com)

"Unapologetically herself, Logan invites readers to consider God and His Word from angles that are both accessible and ceilingless. *Curious Faith* takes the supernatural and the beautiful and the deep things of God and offers them to the woman, like me, in sweatpants and a topknot."

Sara Hagerty, author of *Every Bitter Thing Is Sweet*

"Logan has bared her heart in this book, and we are all the better for it. *Curious Faith* opened my eyes and mind to all the ways that God can show up in the everyday and how often He is waiting for me to see what He is already doing. A beautiful, moving, and impactful book."

Annie F. Downs, author of *Let's All Be Brave*

"*Curious Faith* is a work of flow and liquid, which is to say: Logan's stories and perspectives are water for a weary and dry landscape. If you are thirsty, come and drink. If you don't know if you are thirsty, come and drink anyway; allow yourself the opportunity to taste drops or even whole glasses of a living beverage. A living beverage that could have you longing for a refill and reimagining the scales and terms of your own life in Christ."

Erika Morrison, author of *Bandersnatch: An Invitation to Explore Your Unconventional Soul*

"Logan Wolfram is a gem. Her capacity to love others, personally connect with and challenge those around her is like none other. *Curious Faith* is nothing short of beautiful and brilliant. Each chapter unwraps layers of God's enormity until you are fully covered with a fresh understanding of His love. Get ready to laugh and cry as you are challenged to see, know, and expect more from God than you ever thought possible."

Wynter Pitts, author and founder of *For Girls Like You* magazine and devotional

"Our God may not be a tidy God, but He is a good one. In *Curious Faith*, Logan Wolfram proves herself an incredible guide for the challenge of walking by faith and living in the midst of the journey. Read this for the curious inspiration we all seek."

Claire Díaz-Ortiz, author, speaker, Silicon Valley innovator

"I thought *Curious Faith* would probably be good, but I had no idea it would be this good!"

Mandy Scarr, Logan's assistant and dear friend

"Logan is one thing definitively: contagious. Whether you're having coffee with her or reading her book, her fresh insights and passion are bound to rub off on you. Let her courageous and curious faith rub off on you through these pages. Be encouraged and inspired, challenged and comforted. Not just by her words, but by the God she so intentionally runs after."

Jess Connolly, author and
owner of *Naptime Diaries*

"Logan is a raw and fearless leader. Her new book, *Curious Faith*, matches the rhythm of her life. She is a rare soul who persistently walks towards the light and leads others to do the same. Read this book. You'll be glad you did."

Dr. John Sowers, author of *The Heroic Path*

Curious Faith

REDISCOVERING HOPE IN THE GOD OF POSSIBILITY

LOGAN WOLFRAM

David C Cook®

transforming lives together

CURIOUS FAITH
Published by David C Cook
4050 Lee Vance View
Colorado Springs, CO 80918 U.S.A.

David C Cook Distribution Canada
55 Woodslee Avenue, Paris, Ontario, Canada N3L 3E5

David C Cook U.K., Kingsway Communications
Eastbourne, East Sussex BN23 6NT, England

The graphic circle C logo is a registered trademark of David C Cook.

The website addresses recommended throughout this book are offered as a
resource to you. These websites are not intended in any way to be or imply an
endorsement on the part of David C Cook, nor do we vouch for their content.

Details in some stories have been changed to protect the identities of the persons involved.

Unless otherwise noted, all Scripture quotations are taken from the ESV® Bible (The Holy
Bible, English Standard Version®), copyright © 2001 by Crossway, a publishing ministry of
Good News Publishers. Used by permission. All rights reserved. Scripture quotations marked
NASB are taken from the New American Standard Bible®, Copyright © 1960, 1995 by The
Lockman Foundation. Used by permission. (www.Lockman.org.); NIV are taken from the
Holy Bible, NEW INTERNATIONAL VERSION®, NIV®. Copyright © 1973, 2011 by
Biblica, Inc.® Used by permission. All rights reserved worldwide. NEW INTERNATIONAL
VERSION® and NIV® are registered trademarks of Biblica, Inc. Use of either trademark
for the offering of goods or services requires the prior written consent of Biblica, Inc.

The author has added italics to Scripture quotations for emphasis.

LCCN 2015949959
ISBN 978-0-7814-1350-3
eISBN 978-1-4347-1004-8

© 2016 Logan Wolfram
Published in association with D.C. Jacobson & Associates LLC, an
Author Management Company. www.dcjacobson.com

The Team: Tim Peterson, Ingrid Beck, Nicci Hubert, Tiffany
Thomas, Jennifer Lonas, Susan Murdock
Cover Design: Amy Konyndyk and Nick Lee
Cover Photo: istockphoto.com

Printed in the United States of America
First Edition 2016

1 2 3 4 5 6 7 8 9 10

122315

To my boys, Walker and Hudson: May you live
ever curious and always hopeful in Christ

Contents

Foreword

It was curiosity that led me to answer the phone from a stranger who was reading one of my ebooks.

It was curiosity that led me to sit on the floor with the stranger-turned-acquaintance under a table at the end of a conference to talk and eat chocolate.

It was curiosity that led me to invite this new friend to my home on a snowy day when her flight was canceled.

It was curiosity that led me to invite her to decorate my home.

It was curiosity that led me to ask her to work with me.

And it was this curiosity that led Logan and me into a deep friendship, one that has been full of laughter, tears, and kinship.

Through these precious years of friendship with Logan, I have been able to witness a deep, curious, abiding faith in the woman who has written the words in this life-giving book.

I have witnessed Logan go through deep heartache and yet hold on fiercely to her God, always believing in the hope that was to come.

I have watched her take on adventure in faraway places—not for herself, but in order to bring the kingdom of God to bear through her faithful service.

And I have been inspired by her generosity—one that gives without any trace of expecting something in return.

Logan is one of the most authentic, generous, faithful, open-the-door-wide-to-possibility souls I know. She is a gift, and her hard-fought wisdom words are a gift to us all.

The other night God covered the moon with an eclipse, and the first person I thought of during that spectacular event was Logan.

For it was by a different covering of the moon—a poignant story you will read in this book—that Logan began to *see* God, His character, His brilliance, His majesty, and the fact that He is indeed a miraculous God who can do anything.

Anything.

And she began to not only see Him but also to *believe* Him— to believe He is the God of possibility and hope and miracles and delight.

It was that covering of the moon that weaved in Logan a profound journey of curiosity … of a willingness to watch God and see Him and trust Him in all life's heartache and adventure and unanswered questions. But mostly, she learned to curiously pursue the *unfolding of hope.*

We are in desperate need of hope.

Everywhere we turn, there are heartache and anger and bitterness. The fact that we live in a twenty-four-hour social media culture means there is always more critique and pain and wickedness to view. We are bombarded with the weight of the world and the brokenness of it all. Voices and questions and accusations are constantly directed at the church and at God, even from those who claim His name. We are all so broken, and when hope dims, our souls dim.

We begin to lose clarity through a muddied lens.

We begin to lose our curiosity and replace it with a burden of heavy doubt.

"Did God really say?" whispers the enemy in our ear. And we lean into the doubt because it feels so real, and we feel that maybe God isn't so good or kind after all. I mean, how could a good God do this or that or let that happen?

I've felt those things and I've heard those slithering whispers. Haven't we all, if we're honest with ourselves?

Logan, through raw vulnerability, takes the dark and the whispers and the secret hurts of our hearts, and she shows us through her own vulnerable stories how to get curious when pain arises and things aren't right. She then holds out her hand of experience, study, and faithful prayer, and she offers us the greatest gift to an aching soul: *hope.*

If you are questioning or in a wounded place or just feeling the dullness of a life that wasn't what you expected, Logan's words will bring you relief and, dare I say, *revival* to your soul. After reading *Curious Faith* you will find yourself wanting to know God more; you will want to have Him tenderly explore the parts of your soul that need healing. Ultimately, you will find freedom in places that have previously been locked up.

As Logan so beautifully says, "God's goodness is a vast river of promise, but if we want to experience it, at some point we have to decide to believe it for ourselves and jump in."

Time to jump.

Sarah Mae, author of Longing for Paris:
One Woman's Search for Joy, Beauty, and
Adventure—Right Where She Is

Introduction

Becoming Curious

Blessed are the curious … for they shall have adventures.

Lovelle Drachman

I want you to know before we get into this that I'm not uber-qualified to tell you anything important. I'm a regular gal who is your neighbor, your sister, and your friend. I've thrown an egg at my husband in a moment of insanity, and I've accidentally taught my kids cusswords. I've walked brokenness and pain, and I won't dare ever say that my hurt can even compare to yours. I don't have a gorgeous quiet time with the Lord in the morning light every single day, and I'm not always grateful for the blessings that I know flow abundantly over me. I kick and scream and resist pain just like everyone else. The depravity of my humanity is ever close, which I guess in the end makes me pretty normal.

Over the past several years as a ministry leader, I've met so many women who are intimately acquainted with brokenness and struggle too. Many of you were or are still wrestling to get through the same kinds of hardships I've experienced. My qualifications for writing this book are more acquainted with ADD than with an MD or a PhD, but I *can* tell you that I know what it's like to be broken. But I also know what it is to walk in freedom. The more I have discovered God and curiously pursued Him, the more I've seen Him rewrite my story, dreams, and purposes. I have pressed hard into my God and my faith to now carry hope as the banner over my life. I invite you, in these pages, to do the same.

When Mrs. Buchanan, my Sunday school teacher, led me in a prayer to invite Jesus into my heart, I was nine years old. She told me then that all the angels in heaven were celebrating my decision. I went home that night and repeated the prayer again out the window of my room. Just to be sure it worked the first time.

Life after that mostly felt the same as before. I was reasonably smart and childishly disobedient, and more often than I'd care to admit, I talked back to my parents. But all in all, I was a pretty good kid. I never did anything super crazy. I went on mission trips with my church and had a crush on the boy in my youth group who I thought loved Jesus most of all. Once I told someone that if I had to describe my family, I'd say we were kinda like the Cleavers from *Leave It to Beaver*—mild mannered, loving, typical.

Life was pretty tidy, and God was too. That's the beauty of youth, isn't it? So much of life can appear to be tied up in a box with a pretty bow.

I fit pretty comfortably into a box of expected behaviors and moral decision making. I surrounded myself with plenty of nice people, engaged in reliable philanthropy, and took very few risks. As long as I was going to church and wasn't smoking, drinking, or having sex, I was in the clear to maintain status quo as the nice Christian girl everyone knew me to be. I enjoyed my tidy life and the predictable God I carried with me in a zipped-up, denim-covered Bible to church on Sundays and Wednesdays.

Somewhere around about high school, though, I guess I got bored with that version of the God-of-not-much-personally-impactful and decided that just a little bit of beer and cigarettes and whatever else was probably fine. As long as a thin pair of Fruit of the Looms stayed between me and the boy du jour, that would keep my good-girl status reasonably intact. After all, I knew that Jesus loved me and figured that a few sins could still likely fit inside the box with my tidy God and me.

My days in college were spent at the Baptist Student Union on Wednesday nights and the Sigma Nu house on Fridays and Saturdays. I got good grades, served in student government, enjoyed being the twelfth Kappa Delta in my family, and managed to straddle the fence of my tidy and uneventful faith for most of my college career.

Funny thing about straddling fences, though: eventually you end up with a pain in the butt and not much ground covered in any direction.

CHOOSING HOPE

Whether you're sitting on a fence of faith or forging trails to either side, well, life really doesn't stay tidy for long, does it? Eventually mess happens and the rubber of faith meets the road of living. At some point you become either the broken redeemed or just plain broken.

The qualification that I give to you for writing this book now is that I know my own brokenness, and I know a Redeemer who came to lift me out of it. I know there's a light at the end of the tunnel, and I know that our God is bigger and better than we could ever imagine. I choose that. I choose hope, and I choose to follow.

If you want to see more hope and possibility, though, you have to be willing to look around. You have to be curious.

I love that word because to me it speaks of hope, movement, and limitless possibility. However, being curious means you have to ask hard questions that may or may not yield satisfactory answers. You also have to be willing to walk into places you've never been.

Believe me, it's not any sort of foolish bravery that has led me down these roads. It's a hunger and a curiosity to discover the God of the Bible, who is living and active. I was so tired of my predictable faith that I began to pursue a curious one.

Walking by faith and not by sight has to be curious, right? Close your eyes, walk around, and see where you end up. I bet it won't be where you think. Maybe it'll be even better.

So I choose curiosity because I know that what I have the opportunity to spend a lifetime pursuing and discovering is worth it. God is worth a curious pursuit … even if I'm a hot mess in the process.

Do you wonder about God? Do you wonder where He could take you if you just let go and followed? Are you willing to walk with a curious faith?

It's my hope that within these pages we can journey together. That we can hold hands and expand the parameters of our faith. I want to uncover what a curious faith is in the first place. As we walk side by side, we'll see how we get in our own way and prevent ourselves from living the lives we never dare to dream. We're born with an innate curiosity that compels us to explore, marvel, and believe there is more to life. I want to spend some time digging deeper into the ways that our fears, worries, unmet longings, and losses can rob us of our capacity to live out the hope of Christ.

Curious faith is about rescuing the *now*.

Together we'll realize the possibilities with a God who is unlimited, unpredictable, and ever loving. In these pages I invite you to overcome feelings and outside circumstances that inhibit growth and rob you of hope. I want to be your companion as we figure out how to curiously pursue the wonder of an open-handed life.

I don't want us to just be curious *about* God; I want us to be curious *for* more of Him. I believe that the goodness and wonders of God can amaze us, but it's our curiosity for more of Him that propels us forward to experience more of His presence in our lives. I want to reach beyond merely understanding into the forward movement of curiously pursuing Him.

A MOUNTAINS GIRL

It's easy to see examples of God's faithfulness and creativity in the natural world. Mostly we look around and are able to enjoy what we see.

I grew up in western North Carolina. I guess I've always felt lucky to have spent most of my life pretty close to the mountains and not too far from the beach either. I've always thought this place I live is ideal in so many ways. It's the best of both worlds, just enough of this and that—culture and nature colliding in one geographical area.

As I've grown, the Blue Ridge Mountains still call me back. I'm a mountains girl, and they're home for me. Even if I could escape them, I wouldn't.

Year after year I long to drive the winding roads, windows rolled down, bluegrass music on the stereo, and the smell of mountain laurel and damp moss filling my lungs. I feel alive watching the golden light of late afternoon paint hills whose leaves blaze red and gold and orange in the middle of autumn. And no matter how many times I sit in the same spot on the same porch overlooking the same mountains, it always takes my breath away. I sit in awe of all I see stretching before me. Rocking back and forth, just breathing in the wonder of such beauty.

C. S. Lewis said, "We do not merely want to *see* beauty, though, God knows, even that is bounty enough. We want something else which can hardly be put into words—to be united with the beauty we see, to pass into it, to receive it into ourselves, to bathe in it, to become part of it."[1]

As beautiful as this world is, as much as the wonder of it takes my breath away, it's as if that's still not enough. I want more than that. I want to see myself in it all. How do I fit into the moss, the leaves, and the crisp mountain air?

I don't only want to see new life that springs from the ground of burned forests. I want to know that newness can be for me too. I'm not satisfied with merely viewing vast stars that sprinkle black nights with tiny lights. I want to examine them. I want to break out my dad's old telescope and discover them. I want more than the glow of a moon from where I stand. I want to zoom in, to explore the craters, to see more of what is out there. The beauty is the proof of God all around me, but I want to be united with all of it somehow … to become a part of it, to experience the power behind it all.

Our heavenly Father is a giver of good gifts. He outdoes Himself season after season before our eyes. Harsh winters eventually yield newness of spring. Where we watch leaves dry up and fall to the ground in autumn, a few months later, we see the budding of new growth. Where there has been death, God breathes in life. Things that are broken are made new. The very story of redemption plays out in the world around us. Tiny shoots grow into strong trees when they're rooted deeply in the earth beneath them. The power of God on display in the world invites us to experience the same bits of death and new life ourselves. The rooting of mighty oaks beside rushing waters invites us to curiously imagine the same nourishing life for ourselves. Scripture echoes this thought:

> Blessed is the man who trusts in the LORD,
>   whose trust is the LORD.
> He is like a tree planted by water,
>   that sends out its roots by the stream,
> and does not fear when heat comes,
>   for its leaves remain green,
> and is not anxious in the year of drought,
>   for it does not cease to bear fruit.
>   (Jer. 17:7–8)

Examples of God's faithfulness blanket the earth in beauty and wonder. And while standing in wonder of all that I see takes my breath away, it's my curiosity for more that drives me back time and again.

I sit in the same spot on the same porch, autumn after autumn, noting what is the same and what is different. Every year it seems as if I say, "*This* year is the most brilliant! I've never seen the leaves so bright." Every season I find myself moved in new ways by the vast goodness that surrounds me and curious about how much more of it could be for me.

I watched a documentary about Mount Everest with my kids on Netflix one afternoon. It was a day when homeschool felt exasperating, and I resolved that subjects like science and history could reasonably be checked off by watching an educational film. As I listened to the stories of training for months in advance, arriving and setting up camp at the base of the mountain, and finally the days it takes to climb to the summit, I was intrigued that very few stories being told actually had to do with the end result.

Life happens on the side of the mountain. In the film, the adventure began in the valley and happened on the mountainside. The summit of Everest was incredible, but interestingly enough, at the summit the air is so thin that it can't actually sustain life. No trees grow on the top, and only some of the most fit, strongest-lunged explorers in the world can stand there for any length of time. The summit is a destination to reach, but it's not the spot to live. The richness of the stories that unfolded, well, they happened along the way. So perhaps we're all really mountains people.

Mountains are often like that, aren't they? Whether the mountains are real or metaphorical, the best lessons are learned on the journey. It's as if God knew we needed the world around us to understand the ways we're called to live in pursuit of Him. While the mountaintops may give us great views and perspective, it's the valleys that are most fertile and good for growth. The low points are the spaces that so often make way for the greatest fruit.

But we long for more. We long to see the view from the mountaintop. We want the perspective gained when we stare back down the steep terrain we just scaled and see from whence we came. And while I'm sure we'd appreciate the view if a helicopter plopped us at the top of a great mountain, we'd never appreciate it the same way we would if we conquered the climb ourselves.

So we take our messes and our mountainsides and ask God to make them a beautiful journey. I believe that just as He makes the deadened trees of winter teem with the newness of spring, He can do the same in our lives. He can take rocky bottom places and bring hope, and the broken can be made whole. He takes our doubts and speaks life to them. And somewhere in the midst of it all, instead of just standing in awe, looking at the beauty God creates, we begin to move in curiosity to inhabit that same kind of beauty ourselves.

Let's explore how we can chase after the God who orders the stars. Let's open our eyes wide to the heavens and experience the kingdom of God with childlike wonder. Let's stop trying to control our lives and start living them with a hunger for heaven.

PART 1

Uncovering Curiosity

Chapter 1

The God Who Covers the Moon

I have found it very important in my own life to try to let go of my wishes and instead to live in hope. I am finding that when I choose to let go of my sometimes petty and superficial wishes and trust that my life is precious and meaningful in the eyes of God something really new, something beyond my own expectations begins to happen for me.

Henri J. M. Nouwen, *Finding My Way Home*

"It's not blinking," I said, turning to look for answers in Dr. Keller's eyes. "It's not blinking. What does that mean? It's not blinking. The heart isn't blinking."

My voice was more hurried each time I repeated the sentence. Eyes glued back on the ultrasound screen, I felt numb with the tingles of a million nerve endings. In shock I said it again, this time waiting for Dr. Keller to tell me I wasn't seeing the same thing she was seeing.

"It's not blinking. It's not blinking …"

Dr. Keller's chair squeaked as she turned to face me lying there, feet in the stirrups, eyes frozen forward, heart searching for answers.

There was no flutter of a heartbeat on the screen in front of me. Only stillness.

Tears welled up as she looked at me, her mouth forming the words I didn't want to believe: "Sweetie, I'm so sorry. This just happened. From the looks of things, it was within the past twenty-four hours. I'm so sorry, but the baby has died."

The room went still, and my forward-moving life screeched to a halt. Time and space hovered above me, and everything seemed to be suddenly in slow motion. I'm not sure I was breathing. Half-naked on the table, I lay motionless as the ultrasound tech wiped the cold gel from my swollen belly. They would give my husband, Jeremy, and me some time to process the news before discussing next steps, since I was just entering my second trimester.

We scheduled a D & C for the following Tuesday. It all felt like a blur of heartache and physical sickness. I knew a girl who had the same thing happen, and when she went back before the procedure, the baby's heart was beating again. Maybe this was a fluke. By Monday morning, surely everything would be okay. I held on to hope, fear, and denial in equal parts throughout the weekend.

There was no heartbeat on Monday morning. The screen was still again, and my uterus was clearly collapsing around the tiny frame inside. I stared at the picture before me, as this new salt spilled heavy on the wounds of my brokenness.

On Tuesday I was wheeled into an operating room as a kind nurse leaned over me repeating, "I'm right here. I won't leave you."

Is that You, God? I wondered. The words came out of the nurse's mouth but felt as if they could have been His.

Fat tears trailed down my cheeks as a mask was placed over my nose and mouth. Giant lights hung above me as a team of doctors and nurses moved quickly and spoke in hushed tones. I began breathing in and out, counting, "One ... two ... three ... four ..."

The next thing I remember was waking up, warm blankets around me, nothing left to hold but an empty womb.

ODONTOCHONDRODYSPLASIA IS A FANCY WORD FOR "SOMETHING IS WRONG"

I sat curled with a blanket in the corner of the mossy chenille sofa in our den. It was midafternoon the day after the D & C that left my womb empty, and I was expecting a call from my close friend Emily to learn the gender of her baby. She was eight weeks ahead of me, so she and her husband were at the doctor that morning to find out if they'd be buying clothes in pink or blue. Despite my own pain, I anticipated the excitement of her news.

The phone rang, and the caller ID showed Emily's number. "There's something really wrong," she said. "They're sending us to the high-risk specialist right now. Something is really wrong. It's a boy ... but something is really wrong!"

"It's a boy" was overshadowed by "something is really wrong." In the space where I'd expected the cloud hovering over my spirit to part for just a few seconds, now it began to feel as though a new storm was rolling in over my life.

My insides curled again. It was too much. Not something wrong with her baby too. I pulled the covers into my face and wept hard into the soft fibers.

It took a few days, but eventually we learned that Emily's baby had what the doctors called *odontochondrodysplasia*. The short explanation was a form of dwarfism that caused the baby's rib cage to be too small. They said it didn't appear that his ribs would be wide enough to house his eventually full-grown lungs. Perhaps they wouldn't even be wide enough to expand for a first breath outside the womb. It was a fatal diagnosis, with only about eight recorded cases in history. The doctors said that Emily would probably go full term, but their hopes for the baby's survival were virtually nonexistent.

I remember the day Emily went to choose a burial site and gown, preparing for the end of the tiny life that continued growing inside her. We all spent the next few months praying and preparing for the moment when it would all be over.

Just five minutes, Lord? Aren't You the God of miracles? became the cry of our hearts. A prayer simply that our friends might hold their baby alive.

In the face of Emily's hardship on top of my own, I couldn't deny it anymore: there was nothing tidy about this life we were living.

A MESSY LIFE

The month after our baby died and Emily received her horrible news, my husband and I left the church I had attended for eleven years. After more than a year of feeling like we were swimming the wrong way in the river that was our church, we finally admitted that we needed a change. We felt the tensions of some leadership struggles and watched as a handful of friends were wounded in the wake of a reckless few. We knew too much, and the places God was leading us personally weren't fitting nicely anymore into the way the church body at large was moving.

Eventually we found ourselves paddling against the current of that particular river and knew that for everyone to be healthy, we were the ones who needed to map a different course.

We left the church as well as we knew how, but still, ripping ourselves away from the familiar place where my growing faith was nurtured left a gaping wound for me. Life seemed to be dragging me through the mud, and I was tired of getting dirty.

Next to losing babies, leaving a church may be the hardest thing I've ever done. People take offense and think that the shift in your own walk with God is a commentary on their faith in Him. I swear, some even worried that Jeremy and I were walking away from God altogether. But the truth was that more than ever, we found ourselves desperately pursuing Him. So we walked out of the doors of our church and straight into what turned out to be a period of prolonged hardship in our life.

We wandered around looking for a church home and grasping for straws to hold on to relationships I knew were slipping away. I was drowning in the ache of loss and felt stripped down to raw exposure. Everything in me felt cracked, broken, and lonely. I knew that God had to be near, but still somehow His goodness felt distant.

A few years before our tidy life got really messy, we refinished a dresser for my firstborn's nursery. It was my childhood dresser and was an ugly color. My husband spent weeks stripping off old layers of yellowed varnish before he finally put coat after coat of fresh stain and oil on it to bring out the beauty of the original wood. I felt like that dresser in those days when life got messy—stripped, layer upon layer, until I lay there naked and vulnerable. I hardly knew who I was after losing my church, my friendships there, and that baby.

A CURIOUS AWAKENING

Two months later, on a cold night in February 2008, wiping the remains of dinner from the kitchen counter, I glanced out the window and noticed that something felt different. I moved to lean against our glass door to get a better view of what caught my attention. Instead of the usual powdery, white sphere hanging above, this night's moon was a fiery orb glowing in the sky. Tangerine-colored particles danced in the cosmos as the sun, moon, and earth aligned in a lunar eclipse.

Out of nowhere, the thought rang clear in my mind: *God just covered the moon!*

My mind danced around on the idea as I stood there, face pressed against the cold glass, eyes focused upward into the dark night sky.

God just covered the entire moon. He moved the solar system into alignment and allowed us see it from way down here. God just covered the moon!

I knew there were scientific explanations for a lunar eclipse. But as I believed even then, God is the one who sets everything into motion anyhow. In that moment I realized that the tidy God I had always known wasn't the God He actually is.

I picked up the phone and dialed Emily's number with reckless assurance. She had to see this. She had to see God covering the entire moon.

When Emily answered, I hurriedly said, "Look outside." As I spoke the words into the receiver, my eyes never moved from the glow hanging in the night sky.

"Do you see that? God just covered the moon. He lined up the sun and the earth and covered the moon. I don't know why, but I believe your baby is going to live. I think you will get to hold Cohen alive." I was speaking rapidly now. "God just covered the whole entire moon. How much smaller to heal a baby than to cover the whole moon? I don't know why, but I think Cohen will live."

The audacity of that phone call still shocks me today. I know it sounds ridiculous to dial up a mother with a fatally diagnosed pregnancy and tell her that everything was going to be okay just because the moon was orange. I couldn't help it, though. Something in me broke free when I watched God align the heavens from my spot leaning against the glass door that night. He turned the moon the reddish orange of all the sunrises and sunsets that ring our world at any given moment, and I finally realized that if He could cover the moon, surely He could do anything.

DESPERATE FOR MORE

Do you believe that? That God can do anything? Move mountains? Calm waters? Align planets? Change your life?

How do we connect with a God who can cover the moon one day and yet stand by seemingly idle the next day while our world rips itself apart? The same God who covers the moon and aligns planets also speaks to storms and raging seas. Maybe you're thinking, *Well, then, He also shakes tectonic plates that topple buildings to the ground with people trapped inside. What do you say to that, Logan? If God is truly omnipotent and all-powerful, then surely He can start and stop whatever He wants! If He can, then why does He allow what He allows? Doesn't it make you wonder if He really is as powerful as the Bible says? If He really is good?*

Of course it does. Of course we wonder. But the fruit of the knowledge of good and evil isn't the same as the fruit of understanding. Last time I checked, Adam and Eve got the boot from the garden of Eden before they had the chance to eat more than that one revealing fruit.

The brokenness and devastation on this planet don't fit into a tidy, man-made box any more than a powerful God does. The battle that rages between good and evil simply feels bad. And we can't fix it. So the question becomes, if God *can*, then why doesn't He?

It's interesting how we neuter God of His power when He doesn't always apply it to what we believe is best … or good. And if He doesn't apply His capabilities in the ways we want, I think over time we forget that He still carries that power.

When we see enough hard things in this world, maybe some piece of us decides that perhaps God just can't handle things. So we lose our curiosity about Him. We lose our hope. Eventually we don't really believe that "all things are possible" like the Bible says (Matt. 19:26). A curious faith in a limitless God that we might have had as children is replaced in adulthood with an explainable faith bound by limited possibility.

If God's power doesn't address what we want, then somewhere along the line, we decide that maybe it isn't actually real. Before long we live out our lives from a place where we expect everything to be limited. And the things that fall outside those limits are often beyond repair. Marriages break, cancer steals life, children suffer disease, finances drain, and our spirits are crushed. The God who could do something must not really be able to fix those things after all. Worry, fear, wandering, waiting, and pain become staples that cripple us from living lives full of hopeful anticipation. Sure, there are still good things along the way, but the hallmark of our faith becomes more about managed survival than hope-filled thriving. We're content to live status quo instead of on the edge of limitless possibility. Life is a predictable journey that very rarely surprises anyone, least of all us.

If God really is powerful, if He really is good, then why can't we see it? Maybe we miss what could be right in front of us.

When I watched God cover the moon from my kitchen that February night, something within me shifted. As I was looking out my back door, He put His power on display for me to witness. An orange reminder suspended above that whispered of hope and change. It was an eclipse not just of the heavens but of my heart. As God covered the moon, He *uncovered* my own curiosity and desire for more of Him. In that moment I realized there was a whole lot of God I didn't know. There was a power and a gentleness I was missing. I perceived tiny pieces of Him I'd never seen before but wanted to experience. Since then, everything about my faith has been different.

Perhaps it was that I had already lost so much and was looking for hope. I don't know. What I do know is that once the thought occurred to me that God was rearranging the cosmos before my very eyes, I wanted to know what else He could do. My curiosity about Him began to grow, and I was hungry for the God who moves planets and mends broken hearts. Because if He can cover the moon, the brokenness of this world pales in comparison.

I became ravenously curious for the things of God and heaven. Desperate to see the God who fed five thousand people with only a few morsels, I was determined that there had to be more than the tame faith I had ascribed to for most of my life. I didn't want a tidy God anymore … a God who just bandages wounds and kisses boo-boos. I wanted the God who conducts a planetary orchestra.

I began to ask God for crazy things. I wanted to see miracles and redemption. I wanted to hear Him in ways I never had and see His glory crying out from the side of a mountain. If the people of God don't cry out His majesty, Scripture says the rocks will (see Luke 19:40). I wanted to see all of it. I wanted to live eyes wide open, seeing the God who is in everything.

DEFINING A CURIOUS FAITH

Curiosity to understand the world around us has driven innovation for centuries. From the Romans to Einstein to modern technology and advances, our curiosity for what we don't understand pushes us forward. And whether or not we take hold of the things we pursue, we still press on to chase after increased understanding and attain more of what we're after. We hold on to what has been learned and push into boundaries beyond the known. It's the way of innovation. It's the path of advancement. We apply our curiosity to science, art, business, and technology. And as a general application, we tend to explore areas of societal advancement with more gusto than we do the areas of our own souls.

But this too is how we can develop a deeper faith. We need to explore life and God with the same kind of curiosity to uncover hope along the way.

We can't have a conversation about definitions without including our friend, the Merriam-Webster dictionary, which defines *curious* as "having a desire to learn or know more about something or someone." But when we're talking about faith, I think the apostle Paul said it in Philippians better than Webster or I ever will:

> Not that I have already obtained this or am already perfect, but I press on to make it my own, because Christ Jesus has made me his own. Brothers, I do not consider that I have made it my own. But one thing I do: forgetting what lies behind and straining forward to what lies ahead, I press on toward the goal for the prize of the upward call of God in Christ Jesus. Let those of us who are mature think this way, and if in anything you think otherwise, God will reveal that also to you. Only let us hold true to what we have attained. (3:12–16)

A curious faith is a mobile one. And understanding is an action verb that unfolds before us, as the psalmist declared:

> Your testimonies are wonderful;
> therefore my soul keeps them.

The unfolding of your words gives light;
it imparts understanding to the simple.
(Ps. 119:129–130)

To pursue God is a lifelong exploration that has no end. Maybe it feels laborious to you to know that the journey is never done. But couldn't it be exciting too? To know there is always more to be found? That there's always more goodness and possibility to discover along the way? That a walk with God is always revealing, always uncovering?

An unfolding isn't an immediate reveal; it's a process God invites us to experience with Him. Hold on to what God reveals and know that there is more for you. Press on, friend. Live curious.

Chapter 2

Abandoning a Boxed-Up God

*Much of what we give God credit for today
could be done by the Kiwanis Club.*

Bill Johnson

"Do you see that? God just covered the moon.... I don't know why, but I believe your baby is going to live."

Whatever led me to call Emily the night of the lunar eclipse with such a bold declaration of faith still shocks me. Where did I get off calling and saying things like that? What kind of friend—or idiot—makes proclamations of hopes that have no medical foundation? I hung up and realized that either I was full to the brim with a newfound faith in a God of amazing possibility, or I was a total jerk.

But now my God had covered the moon, and I couldn't ignore it. And I figured that if He could cover the moon, and create life, then surely He could expand rib cages long enough for Emily to have her five minutes with her newborn son, Cohen—or maybe even more.

I went by myself to the hospital to see Emily one night in early March. Preeclampsia had forced the issue of birth three weeks early, and she let me know she was going in for an emergency C-section.

The sky was overcast, but I could still see the white light of the moon shining in the night sky as I walked through the hospital parking lot. A gust of wind blew, and the edge of the glowing orb peeked out from behind the feathery clouds. The same God who had just a month before aligned the earth and sun with this moon was now obstructing it with congregating vapors in the heavens. It was the same moon that had always been hanging there in the sky, but this time it felt as if the face in it was speaking directly to me.

The God Who Covers Moons was looking down on my friends, and all I could hear Him saying was, "How much smaller to heal a baby than to cover the whole moon."

I walked into a corner room in the hospital, where a large group was waiting for the news of Cohen's birth. Dr. Keller passed me in the hallway, and her kind eyes conveyed that she understood this was a hard place for me to be for so many reasons. The last time I'd seen her was when she emptied my own broken womb a few months earlier.

I entered the room full of friends and other people I'd known for years. Wading through the polite exchanges, I found a seat on the floor beside my friend Kelley. We marveled that the moment had finally arrived. But no one really knew what to say. All I could think was that we needed to be praying.

I suspect that most everyone there felt completely inadequate for the situation. It was all very heavy. Months of worry and fear now culminated in one final moment of birth, and all we really knew to do was to be there.

But something in me felt unsettled and annoyed by the nervous surface chatter filling much of the room. This was our moment to intercede. This was our last shot to kneel before God and beg for the miraculous. Maybe everyone thought it was too late. I don't know. This was it, though ... the time to be born and die all at once. And everyone just stood around waiting to see how long it would last.

Suddenly a group of people I didn't know walked into the room together. With a purpose in their steps, they filed into the center of the room. Then a man stepped up and broke the hum of conversation, confidently saying, "Let's all circle up and pray together."

I crossed my legs beneath me on the plum-colored, commercial carpet, and my elbows pressed forward into my thighs. My hair fell over my face as I pushed the heels of my hands into my eyes to keep from crying. People in conversations around the edges of the room turned to face the center.

I started to silently repeat in my mind, *You are the God who covers moons ... You are the God who covers moons ... You are the God who covers moons.*

Popcorn prayers began littering the room around me, but there seemed to be a sense of resignation in the voices. Why were we merely praying for comfort in this time of grief when the baby wasn't even born yet? Why were we asking for an understanding of the death of a baby who was still very much alive? Why weren't we all praying beyond what seemed possible?

No! Just no, God! If this is You, then I don't know if I want You anymore, my spirit cried out to heaven.

I opened my mouth and prayed for life in Emily's womb that didn't seem possible. Without the intervention of a moon-covering God that I felt sure was real, Cohen didn't stand a chance.

But then I heard a voice in the room begin to pray. It was the man who had first spoken. "Lord, we ask that even as we speak, Cohen's rib cage would expand. Father, in the name of Jesus, we declare healing over this baby. Almighty God, we pray that even as they lift him from the womb, the pictures on the ultrasound machine wouldn't match the extended limbs and healthy body they hold in their hands. We are asking You, Lord, for the miraculous!"

Other voices rang out in affirmation.

Yes! Who are these people? I wondered. *How is it that they even know to pray like this? Maybe they know something about the moon-covering God too. They must ... they must.*

After we finished praying, I walked up to the man, inserting myself into the conversation. I was desperate to know more.

"Who are you, and where did you learn to pray like that?" I asked. "How do you know this about God? What do you know that I don't know? Where can I learn more?"

I peppered him with questions and frantically told him about the lunar eclipse that rocked my bland theology just a few weeks earlier. He invited me to a weekly prayer meeting the following Monday. But before I could ask any more questions, a nurse came into the room with incredible news. Cohen had been born, and he was breathing on his own. Chris and Emily were holding him!

He was breathing ... on his own!

I stood in wonder and awe of my vast and powerful God, and a desire for more of His goodness moved my heart with wild abandon after Him. Sitting there on what could have been another rock bottom, I felt things looking up. When God covered the moon, creation had begun to teach me that my view of Him was far too small. He wasn't just a civil servant; he was a powerful and loving Creator. A fresh understanding of Him was set in motion, and the tidy, stagnant theology that had marked most of my life started edging curiously forward. As I found myself in awe of Him, hemmed into safe places with Him from top to rock bottom, I began to discover freedom to wonder and to be curious about what He could have for my life. I took the sides off the box I'd spent a whole lifetime fitting around God. And suddenly I didn't want to contain Him anymore.

TIDY FAITH, CIVIC GOD

I'd never seen a miracle before. Remember, I grew up with that tidy faith, keeping life in sensible boxes. Things like healing and prophecy and the miraculous I'd learned were for a different time and place. Those things were for an age that was written about thousands of years ago and recorded by men in robes who lived when crucifixion and stoning took care of public problems. Never mind that unexplainable things also made me feel completely uncomfortable. God, who is supposedly the same God He was back then, operates within cleaner and more easily explained boundaries in this present era. I needed explanations for things to keep them in order.

The tidy God I'd always happily believed in didn't have much more power to institute change than any solid civic organization, like the Rotary Club, Kiwanis, or Shriners. Don't get me wrong; they all do wonderful things, such as raising money to fight disease, providing scholarships for underprivileged children, investing in community-enhancing projects. But it's all within a limited capacity. Somewhere along the way, I lost sight of the God who orders the heavens. I ascribed civic helpfulness to Him and forgot about the magnitude and love of a Creator who sent His Son to die on a cross for me. Rather than pursuing in holy fear the God of inexplicable possibility, I lived with mediocre faith in an impotent God of the easily interpreted human solution.

Blah … blah … boring faith.

I'm not the only one, though, right? I bet you've asked God for things, only to wonder if He's even listening. In a world where we have phenomenal medical advances, technologies to communicate across miles, and the ability to push ourselves to impressive heights, it's easy to put our trust elsewhere. When we see quantifiable results from human efforts, we begin to ask God for only as much as we can make sense of ourselves.

In what ways have you limited God? What in your own life has minimized hope? How has your attitude toward God reduced your faith? Do you carry an offense against Him for your disappointments? If God is good, then why is there so much bad in the world? Perhaps you've been hurt by the church. Or maybe someone who claimed to love God did something horrible to you.

We're all a broken people in need of saving, but do we even believe that God can save us anymore, when we feel that so many times He hasn't? When the harshness of life robs us of a childlike perspective, is it even possible to pursue hope again?

When things we can't explain or understand make us feel uncomfortable or hurt, we forget that they can make us curious too.

ROCK-BOTTOM FAITH

> "It's going to be so cool when I grow up and get
>   fired from my job."
> "One day when I'm big, I'm going to get a divorce
>   and declare bankruptcy!"
> "I can't wait to get married and be widowed when
>   I'm thirty."

Things no child has said, *ever*.

We don't dream dreams about living at low points. When we think of life, none of us want to spend it at the bottom of the barrel, the end of the road, the place where everything sinks and seems to come to a halt. No person ever longs to hit rock bottom. But if we're rethinking the movement of our faith and curiosity for more of God, then we need to also consider how far our theology will allow us to sink. And for all the efforts we make to keep from sinking low, somehow it seems that within each of our lives, we still do.

What is rock bottom? It's the core of the earth, the depths of a soul, seemingly the furthest point we can fall from grace. It's the moment in life when a meth addict realizes she hasn't eaten in two weeks and is sleeping on the dirty floor of a cheap motel surrounded by ten other people in the same mess. It's the businessman who makes a few bad investments and declares bankruptcy, sells his house and cars, loses his family, and moves into an apartment on the other side of town. It's the state of a soul after fighting for the life of a loved one, draining a bank account to seek medical solutions, and spending night after night on bent knees in desperate prayer for healing, only to kiss comatose lips good-bye one last time as a final breath exhales in this world.

Rock bottom is that place where we come to the end of ourselves, and there seems to be nowhere left to go, no further place to fall, no deeper place to sink. It's the place of disappointment and failure that we don't ever dream of finding ourselves in. Perhaps it's even the place we spend a lifetime trying to avoid.

But man, this life is full of disappointments. And for every new stage, there can be a new version of the bottom. What feels like the depths when we're nineteen years old is different from what feels like the end of hope at thirty-five, sixty-five, or ninety.

When I was nineteen, I had a long-distance boyfriend. He was the first person I ever told that I loved, and I spent late college nights on AOL Instant Messenger and the phone to keep in touch. The summer after my sophomore year, I moved to be closer to where he lived and looked forward to finally being able to spend more time together, since we wouldn't have entire states separating us. That summer in Colorado, I was finally just six hours from where he lived, instead of twenty-five. It was close enough for short trips. So in June, when I went to spend Father's Day weekend with his family, I was beside myself, excited to finally be together.

To my surprise, he avoided me the whole weekend and eventually admitted a random fling with a girl back at school. He had become a father a month prior to this confession. When I think back on it, I wish I'd offered him a Father's Day card enveloped in clever detachment and sarcasm. But I'm pretty sure I just sat in silence on the basement couch with tears streaming down my face.

I spent the remainder of the summer far away from home, feeling lonely, abandoned, and betrayed. Would I ever be able to trust anyone again? Would I ever be able to love anyone again? I didn't know. All I knew was that it felt as if I had sunk to the bottom of my own broken heart. Chicago's "I Don't Wanna Live without Your Love" played repeatedly on my stereo, and I cried myself to sleep most nights. Eventually I called my parents and begged them to come get me and bring me home. I wondered how long it would take for me to feel whole again. It was my first taste of what it felt like to hit the bottom.

Many years later I hit rock bottom again as I stared at the stillness of that heart not beating on the ultrasound screen in front of me. For months afterward, any movie or television show I saw with an ultrasound scene sent me into heaving sobs. Each phone call from yet another newly pregnant friend felt like a shot to my own heart. I occupied the end of myself in that place for what felt like a couple of years. I was a mess of despair and brokenness.

My beloved grandfather and patriarch of our family, Bop, died in January 2000. He and Nanny had been married for fifty years the previous summer. They spent a lifetime together, more than twice as long together as apart. I remember how Nanny looked at his funeral: hollow eyes staring into nothing, mouth drawn to contain overwhelming emotion. It appeared as if all life had vacated her physical body. I can't even imagine what the bottom feels like when half of your life is one minute teasing you, and in less time than it takes for you to make your morning cup of coffee, an artery bursts, and you return to the room to find your soul mate dead on the bed. That is a low, low bottom I have yet to fathom.

As we explore new waters of life, we may also discover new depths in those proverbial seas. The further out we go and the deeper we invest in our lives, the lower we can sink when life pushes us under the waves. What feels like drowning at age nineteen so often can't even compare to the ways we gasp for air later in life.

And so we go along, alternating between living high on full lives and sinking low to new depths. There will always be brokenness in this life. We'll always have disappointments. We'll spend time after time picking ourselves up when life spirals us down to rock bottom. We'll see the bottom more times than we ever care to. I'm sorry to say, but you can just about count on it.

This is why it matters so much that we define rock bottom before we ever get there. If we allow our circumstances to dictate how low we sink, there's no telling how far we may fall. Disappointment shuts down our ability to hope and robs us of possibility. We fear being disappointed again, so we stop hoping altogether. It's hard to have a curious faith if we don't develop an understanding of where we land when we hit the bottom. But if we want to really live, then getting to the end of ourselves is actually just the beginning.

So we define rock bottom to shore up our theology, to give us space to move in curiosity. The end, which is really the beginning, is that our great God is good and that He is for us. He hung the moon and stars in the heavens, paints hills in afternoon sunlight, makes dying babies breathe, and absorbed brokenness on a cross so that we may become new creations. If the lowest we ever allow ourselves to sink still proclaims a story of redemption, then even the deepest deep is a springboard for forward movement again.

The depths of emotional oceans, the end of ourselves, the roads that seem to lead nowhere all finish at the foot of a cross sunk deep into the bottom of a rock called Golgotha. And the Man—Jesus— who met His end on that rock is the reason we can all have a new beginning. Because He died in our place, we too can say,

> I have been crucified with Christ; and it is no longer I who live, but Christ lives in me; and the life which I now live in the flesh I live by faith in the Son of God, who loved me and gave Himself up for me. (Gal. 2:20 NASB)

When that vantage point becomes the lowest we can ever sink, everything else will always look up. In dying to ourselves, we truly find life. The apostle Paul discovered this and even rejoiced at rock bottom. At his lowest point in prison, he proclaimed,

> Yes, and I will continue to rejoice, for I know that through your prayers and God's provision of the Spirit of Jesus Christ what has happened to me will turn out for my deliverance. I eagerly expect and hope that I will in no way be ashamed, but will have sufficient courage so that now as always Christ will be exalted in my body, whether by life or by death. For to me, to live is Christ and to die is gain. (Phil. 1:18–21 NIV)

Our God is King of the comeback. No matter what, no matter how hard the winds of life try to blow you down, or whether the depths reach out to drown you, there *is* redemption. The nature of God, His goodness, and His entire plan for the earth are for a comeback. Christ's resurrection more than two thousand years ago means that you can rise again now.

Maybe you feel like something is holding you underwater, pushing you to the bottom. Grab on to your foundation of faith in a good God and push yourself back up. We're not meant to wait helplessly in a broken world, but to make comebacks over and over. So instead of falling into a downward spiral to a rock bottom when life pushes you under, reach out for the foundation of your faith and live out a redemptive push upward season after season.

The end of yourself is the beginning of hope, and defining rock bottom offers new life. Reach out to take hold of your Creator, whose character and capacity beckon you to follow. Sink your foundation into endings that become beginnings, and hold on to hope to follow curiously after the God who pulls you out of the pit to rise again. You can always wonder, always follow, and always pursue curiously after God, who is good and full of hope and possibility.

Chapter 3

A Case of Mistaken Identity

Be yourself; everyone else is already taken.

Attributed to Oscar Wilde

When I was sixteen, I got a really dumb tattoo. I mean, everything about it was totally ridiculous, and these days I'd even go so far as to say almost embarrassing. What was supposed to be a cute ladybug originally intended for my foot somehow ended up being a strange, otherworldly looking insect on my abdomen. (I know, tattoos on abdomens at age sixteen—I clearly didn't consider the repercussions of childbirth on permanent ink.) Said ladybug now looks more like a cockroach that had an unfortunate run-in with the bottom of a foot. Bygones or not, tattoos are *permanent*!

Anyhow, redemption is for us all, right?

A few years later, when I was twenty-two, I thought I'd get some new ink that was more symbolic of my faith. I needed something that was a better self-identifier than a bug. So get this: I googled "Christian symbols" because, of course, that would lead me down a path of deeper meaning, right? Google searches always yield results that are ripe with meaning and truth. Have mercy … the naïveté!

Thanks to a person named Radar at Pain & Wonder (terrifying name, I know) in Athens, Georgia, the seal of Martin Luther is now inscribed on my lower back. (If you didn't know, Luther was an old-school theologian who taught that salvation is a free gift of God.) The Martin Luther seal represented the plan of salvation all in one lovely illustration—death, life, hope, heaven, eternity. It seemed inconspicuous, hidden, personal, and rich with meaning. But when I got married, my husband pretty much immediately exclaimed, "*What?* You have a Christian tramp stamp? How is that even possible? BWAAAHAHAHAHAA!"

And I die. My naive little spirit died a rapid, tiny death in that moment too. I seriously had no idea there was such a phrase. Mortifying! This is what happens when nice Christian girls decide to explore their inner rebel. Is there such a thing as a redeeming tramp stamp? Because, well, maybe it could be a thing.

So anyhow, I watched a movie a few years ago (that, for the record, I don't recommend), and at one point there was a conversation between a man and a really ridiculous boy who had a giant tattoo across his collarbone that read "NO RAGRETS."

The man in the scene looked at all the boy's tattoos and then sarcastically said, "What is this one [on your neck]?"

The boy replied, "Oh, this? This is my *credo*. No regrets."

As he eyed the obvious misspelling, the man smirked and said, "Mm-hmm. You have no regrets? Not even a single letter?"

"No way. Not me!" the boy insisted.[1]

Although our own mistakes may not be so glaringly obvious, I think it's probably fair to say that that ridiculous boy wasn't the first person to ever mislabel something or to be defined in some clearly regrettable way.

Some of us may have an epidermal billboard declaring, "This is who I am." Perhaps for you, it's the way you dress, or the things you post on Facebook, or the attitude you have toward life. There are a million different ways we can display our identity and a zillion different moments that can shape it in the first place. Yet I wonder how often the thing we display for all to see isn't so much our true identity as it is a misspelled word that reveals our own confusion about who we really are.

A MOTHER OF WARRIORS

The week after we lost our first baby, my husband and I went to dinner with some old friends. They cried over our loss and prayed with us as we all grieved together. At one point in the prayer, one of them said to me, "I really feel like the Lord is going to make you a mother of warriors." I'm certain he said more than that, but "mother of warriors" really stood out in my mind.

I don't know why, but those few words stuck with me. They were about who I was and who I would become. They spoke into some need I had to feel like I mattered or counted for something. Those few words made me curious about my future and the plans God could have for me. Perhaps something resonated with me about possibility, potential, or hope for my future.

When I later lost yet another baby and began a go-round with secondary infertility, I started asking God a few questions about those once-encouraging words. I began to lose sight of myself and the things God could have for me. I was broken and messed up. My own body was somehow a baby killer, and I didn't know where that left me in the end. Was I useless? A disaster? A lost cause of motherhood? I simultaneously lost sight of and became consumed by myself. I forgot who I was and the potential I carried simply because Christ lives in me.

So many decisions in my life felt stuck. I was trapped between hope for an indeterminate future and the day to day of living in my present brokenness. Should I even bother trying to shed the unwelcome ten pounds I gained from a fruitless pregnancy in the hopes of being back in maternity clothes soon? Or should I just move on and get rid of the clothes altogether? I lost myself in the motherhood that wasn't coming the way I'd planned, but if I was honest, there were plenty of other ways I'd lost myself long before then.

Maybe you can relate. Rather than reorienting ourselves when we're lost, so often we become paralyzed with indecision and insecurity and just stop moving altogether. Losing myself, I lost my way, and eventually it was as though I just sat down and stopped moving forward in pursuit of anything at all. When I lost myself, I lost my curiosity to even pursue God.

One day in church I cried out to Him, *Who am I, God? I'm the mother of one child, and "warriors" is plural. If not this, then who am I?* It felt as if the purposes I thought He had for me would never come to fruition.

In that moment I had a sense that God wanted to do something great through my husband. *You are the wife of a general in My army. I want to do great things for My kingdom through your husband.* I felt proud and grateful for this new word over my life. I tucked it into my heart, and it seemed to be enough for a while.

A couple of years later, I gave birth to our second son. Then after some time passed, we decided to try for another baby, you know, to fill my minivan. I walked confidently and without worry into my fifth pregnancy until a third miscarriage caught me completely off guard.

What the crap, God? Seriously, "warriors" is a plural word, which indicates to me more than two! I thought our family would look different than this. I had dreamed of a big, bustling houseful of kids. So I ask You again, God, WHO AM I? Mother of warriors and the wife of a general is all well and good. But what if they all died? What if they were taken from me; then who would I be? What would be left of me? Who am I without anyone else?

It wasn't audible, but God's voice rang clear in my heart. *First and foremost, you are a daughter of the King.*

First and foremost, you are a daughter of the King.

About a month later, I got a new tattoo. Let's not dote long on the fact that three weeks after I got this long-researched inking, a similar image showed up on a set of cork coasters at Hobby Lobby. Thank heavens it's no longer appearing in craft stores around the nation with the same frequency, but even if it does, that doesn't matter to me. The antique crown on my arm, which is decorated with four stars and has the words *mother of conquerors* written in Hebrew below, reminds me that my identity and the things I experience in life aren't a mistake. My identity is tied up in who God says I am. (Please know, I don't think this particular method of remembering things is for everyone. But I'm a visual person, and it helps when I see what I don't want to forget.)

For the first two months after getting the tattoo, I kept thinking a spider was crawling on my arm, but now that I'm used to it, the tattoo constantly reminds me of what I so often forget. In my sin and muck, I don't remember who I am. The tattoo is just pictures and symbols, but to me it represents the words that the Lord speaks about me. It's about some roles I fill and, most important, about how God identifies me: "mother of warriors, wife of a general, but first and foremost, a daughter of the King."

Acts 9 tells the story of Saul's radical conversion. Once a violent and renowned persecutor of the followers of Christ, Saul had even gone so far as to ask the religious higher-ups for special permission to pretty much erase the existence of Christians in Damascus, Syria. On his way to fulfill his role, he was thrown to the ground, blinded by a great light, and heard the voice of God speaking directly to him, calling him by name:

> "Saul, Saul, why are you persecuting Me?" And [Saul] said, "Who are You, Lord?" And He said, "I am Jesus whom you are persecuting, but get up and enter the city, and it will be told you what you must do." (vv. 4–6 NASB)

As I read through this familiar passage again, I was startled to realize that Saul was actually blind for three full days. Scripture says his eyes were open, but he couldn't see. The men who were with Saul had to lead him "by the hand" into the city (v. 8 NASB). Their initial plan was derailed by this detour plan that the Lord dropped on them in the middle of the road. They didn't even know what they were supposed to do when they got to Damascus. Can you imagine the confusion?

Jesus told Saul, "Get up and enter the city, and it will be told you what you must do."

So we have this guy pursuing the life he thought he was called to lead, when he suddenly had a radical encounter with the Lord. He was blinded and led to a place where he had no idea what he was supposed to do next. And by the way, he also ended up with a new name. "Saul the zealot" became "Paul the apostle," and the purposes he carried before shrank into the past as God identified him in a new way. Interestingly enough, he had gotten so skewed in his thinking that he thought he was protecting the very thing he was, in fact, tearing down. He lost sight of his identity as a child of God and had to be abruptly interrupted and reminded to course-correct.

When Ananias revealed God's plans to Saul, the Lord said, "[Saul] is a chosen instrument of Mine, to bear My name before the Gentiles and kings and the sons of Israel" (v. 15 NASB).

Seems I'm not the only one who has ever lost sight of my true identity. Saul was such a hot mess that even God Himself had to tell the people around him what His purposes were for the man.

Saul had a whole lot of reasons to live with a case of mixed-up identity. "Who am I, Lord?" he could have asked when he lost sight of who he was or what he was doing there on that Damascus road.

But no, what Saul spoke into the air that day was, "Who are *You*, Lord?" (v. 5 NASB). He knew that somehow his identity was wrapped up in this voice from the sky that obstructed his own plans. The One who interrupted those plans was the same One who would give Saul a new purpose and a new name.

"Get up and enter the city, and it will be told you what you must do."

We may think we're on one road doing one thing. We allow outside circumstances to tell us who we are and define our purpose and value. But then God stops us dead in our tracks, removes our ability to see where we're going, and tells us to walk a ways farther, with no clue where we're headed. Maybe, just maybe we get over ourselves, because God wants to take us to a new place with a new name and a new purpose that we won't know until we get to wherever He is leading us.

The identity that the Lord has for me is clear, even if His plans for my life aren't. He calls me by name, redeems the regrettable in my life, and gives me new purpose.

I hope you're smarter than the boy in the movie and don't have "RAGRETS" engraved on your body. But I'll bet you have a few regrets written on your life.

It doesn't matter what seemingly permanent things you've inked onto your heart about who you are or who you think you are. That's because God in His kindness redeems our misguided markings. In His goodness, He frees us from the messes we make and renames and rebrands us. He doesn't allow the scarlet letters we emblazon on our chests to be the things that define us. Instead, He tells us to bind His Word around our necks and write His teachings on our hearts:

> Let not steadfast love and faithfulness
> > forsake you;
> bind them around your neck;
> write them on the tablet of your heart.
> > (Prov. 3:3)

> My son, keep my words
> > and treasure up my commandments
> > > with you;
> keep my commandments and live;
> > keep my teaching as the apple of your
> > > eye;
> bind them on your fingers;
> > write them on the tablet of your heart.
> > > (7:1–3)

The point is, God gives each of us a new name and a new identity to make permanent in our hearts. He defines who we are and doesn't want us to go around living like our identity is unknown. We can't walk in curiosity after God when we have no idea who we are. We can't follow behind when we can't even get our bearings about where we've come from. Who we are isn't wrapped up in what the world says about us or what we do; who we are is in relation to the God of the universe. And He says that we are sons and daughters of the King.

Make no mistake. God doesn't forget our names even when we do:

> Even [your mother] may forget,
>   yet I will not forget you.
> Behold, I have engraved you on the palms of
>   my hands. (Isa. 49:15–16)

Look at those verses! I guess not all permanent ink is regrettable after all, huh?

THE VALUE OF A MASTERPIECE

Recently I came across a Dove soap video produced in France that reduced me to tears. In the clip, women had been asked to record in a journal all the thoughts they had about themselves throughout the day. Dove then turned the women's thoughts into a dialogue that played out at a street café within earshot of several other tables, including the tables where the original women were sitting.

"You have a big chest and short legs. Some women can make that work. But you … you've got no charm. You're just fat and ordinary."

"Every time you smile, those baby teeth you have make you look like a mouse."

"Sit straight up so your belly doesn't look so big."

Strangers overhearing the conversation were appalled to hear the way the women spoke to one another, and they interrupted the exchange.

"That's so violent what you're saying to her! You should stop. Your words are so unkind."

When the original women realized that the words being spoken were the thoughts they had journaled, they were mortified.

"It's so horrifying. I hope my daughter never speaks to herself like that," one woman observed.

I cried my way through the video, realizing that it wasn't just those women. I do it too. So many of us do. Over and over we devalue ourselves. But we cannot walk into our full potential in Christ when we believe that who He created us to be falls woefully short.

How often do we forget our value? How often do we believe the lies of the world instead of the words of our Creator about us? We set aside the truth that Jesus came and lived and died to prove to us that we are of great value to the God of the heavens. Even Dove soap sees our value. Our renowned Creator has given us inherent value. Even so, we call "ugly" what God calls a "masterpiece." And then we operate according to the lies and lose the capacity to follow Him curiously.

How we minimize that ultimate price Jesus paid when we insist that more must be done to redeem our messy lives. We make satan's job so simple. He plants one tiny lie somewhere along the way, and we take it from there all the way to our own self-destruction.

We all have them, those lies we believe. Yet we adopt new ideas that we think will cover them. But eventually the facade cracks, and the old lies are still there … still distorting our beliefs about everything. Instead of moving forward in curiosity after God, we get stuck on lies about ourselves. That's why learning to uncover the lies matters so much. Let's name them. Let's call them out! Let's *stop* believing them and replace them instead with the truth of Christ.

A DEFINING ROLE

I get it, though. We forget what God says about our identity in Him. We get wrapped up in the things around us. Our families require so much of us that we can lose ourselves. Our jobs turn us into people we didn't ever think we'd be. The harsh reality of life exploits and exposes us. So we turn inward and try to protect what little we think remains. We lose our ability to wonder, and then wandering begins to feel like a wilderness. We know there is more to life, but we don't even have the energy to be curious about how to get it. Then one day we wake up lost and don't know how to get back to what or who we used to be.

You aren't what you do. Your profession isn't who you are. You aren't defined by your roles: career woman, wife, mom, sister, brother, husband, et cetera. Those are gifts you have and roles you fulfill. But they don't define the core of your being. You aren't the sum of your mistakes or the messed-up identity you once wore like an albatross around your neck. Your identity is simple. It's clear. It's beautiful. Your identity is purely who God says you are. Beautiful, redeemed, renamed, engraved on the hands of Christ, where you will never be forgotten.

My pastor at church, Tony, recently said that the issues around us can't define how we stand, when we're actually seated with God:

> If then you have been raised with Christ, seek the things that are above, where Christ is, seated at the right hand of God. Set your minds on things that are above, not on things that are on earth. For you have died, and your life is hidden with Christ in God. When Christ who is your life appears, then you also will appear with him in glory. (Col. 3:1–4)

Where we sit determines how we stand. So stand tall, stand true, in honor and dignity and kindness and grace. Wear the self that was made for you. Toss off the raggedy clothes of mistaken identity and put on the "robe of righteousness" that is yours in Christ Jesus:

> I will greatly rejoice in the LORD;
>> my soul shall exult in my God,
> for he has clothed me with the garments of
>> salvation;
>> he has covered me with the robe of
>> righteousness. (Isa. 61:10)

Roles change. Phases of life pass. Jobs shift. Children grow up. Parents die. And if who we are is wrapped up in the people or the things that surround us, we lose sight of ourselves and subsequently how to follow Christ fully. Everything may change around us, but the way God sees us never does.

PRAYING THE OPPOSITE

Several years ago, when I was beginning to crawl out from under the rock of my apocalyptic stage of overwhelming brokenness (losing our church, friends, and babies), I learned about a tool that has reshaped much of the way I know and understand God and my identity in His kingdom.

Of all the things I've read on identity or an orphan spirit, understanding worth, or embracing my value as a daughter of the King of heaven, this exercise redefines my grasp of truth over and over.

I know who God says I am because I ask Him to show me Himself when I forget. And when I forget, or choose to ignore, what He says about other people, I do the same thing.

Some people get real charismaticky and call it "praying in the opposite spirit." But I just call it "praying the opposite" because that makes the most sense to me.

Here's what I mean. When I'm writing, or praying, I've found that I love tools that help me brainstorm other words that expand the way I think about a certain topic. In writing, it's sort of taboo to repeat the same word over and over. So thanks to the Google synonym search, I have loads of options right at my fingertips when the right word is escaping me. If I need another word for *say*, I just type *say* into the search engine and voilà! I have gobs of words to choose from. Suddenly my vocabulary expanded when my brain was stuck. For example, instead of repeating *say*, I now have options like *speak*, *suppose*, *articulate*, *share*, and *tell* to toss into my verbal arsenal.

For opposites, it works pretty much the same way. It's just that instead of synonyms, I think in terms of antonyms.

Sadly, because of our inherently sinful nature, it's easy for most of us to think of a negative something or other. But I figure that if we're going to be nasty, then it's time we grab that sinful nature by the horns and put it to work for forward kingdom movement!

We're all so awesome, right? Always kind, always giving others the benefit of the doubt, never judgmental. Oh, wait, you're not? Whew! Me neither. I bet if I asked you right now to pick the speck out of someone else's eye, you'd do it well before you'd tackle the log in your own. You know what I mean. It's easier to find the little fault in someone else rather than the massive skeletons you've stored up and refuse to deal with in your own closet.

Seriously, right now, this very second, I want you to think about something another person did that ticked you off. Conjure in your mind the thing that grates your nerves and rubs you the wrong way. Think about the thing that made you so mad you had to call your sister to vent while you were putting waffles in the toaster oven at breakfast this morning. The moment that made you put a crooked smear of eyeliner on your lid because when you thought of it, you scrunched your face, and it messed up your application. Think of it now. Think of the name of the person who did it.

For real. Who was it?

Now that we know I'm not the only jerk in the world, let's talk about how to do something good with all of our nasty.

What was the thing that person did? Think of a word or two to describe the offense. Was it pride? Was it selfishness? Was it unkindness or impatience? Name the word. Despite the fact that your face is flushed and you're feeling agitated now, I promise we're going somewhere good here.

Next, think of the opposite of that word. For instance, the opposite of *pride* is *humility*. *Selfishness* converts to *generosity*. *Unkindness* to *kindness*, *impatience* to *patience*. You get my drift.

Once you've defined the opposite for your original word, grab a Bible ... or your smartphone. Put down this book and look up that word, plus other positive words, such as *kindness* or *patience*. Then search for a few scriptures that contain those words.

I'll wait for you to come back....

Okay, I'm assuming you actually did it. So, how'd it go? How do you feel?

I don't know about you, but it's generally easy for me to think of how prideful so-and-so is behaving. Rather than camping out on her nasty qualities, though, I just train myself (most of the time) to apply my little "rule of opposites" to the situation. Instead of asking the Lord to help Patty Prideful to simply overcome her pride, I can cut that yuckiness off at the knees and pray in the blessings of heaven instead. Rather than engaging in a battle, I have access to the benefits promised in Jesus to overcome the yuckiness (both for her and for me). I figure if I can think so fast of ugly things like pride, then I can certainly make my way on over to a blessing of humility from there.

So in the name of Jesus—because He told us to pray in His name—I can ask the Lord to cut out her pride and replace it with humility. Then once the whole humility thing is going, I can begin to think of synonyms and other positive qualities to pray in more blessings. I now consider words like *modesty*, *meekness*, *kindness*, and *gentleness*, and I can pray those added blessings for Patty Prideful as well. Instead of having a holy gossipfest with the Lord—"Jesus, bless Patty's nasty little prideful heart"—I can actually walk away from praying for Patty feeling better about her than worse! "Lord, I bless Patty with humility. I ask that Your kindness would wash over her and that she would understand Your great love for her" … and so on and so forth. Novel idea, right?

Maybe you're thinking, *Logan, this "praying the opposite" exercise is just a bunch of silly self-talk. Because we can't change people by praying for them from a distance. We have to engage with them directly or wait for the Lord to reveal the problem to them, which takes time.*

I'll give you that. Patty might still be horribly prideful, and being around her might often make me want to chew my own arm off. The difference now, however, is that I can influence my own heart by speaking a blessing over her. I've learned to never underestimate the work I'm doing by battling on behalf of Patty in the heavenlies. I may or may not get to see the fruit of a change in her attitude, but I can certainly experience the shift in my own!

It's pretty simple to think about applying that idea to other people. And for me, that was sort of how some of my curious forward movement began. If I was mad at my husband for behaving in a way I perceived to be too harsh, instead of simply gabbing to God about how harsh and mean and unthinking he was being, I could begin to submit those things to Jesus. I could focus on the negative, or I could ask God to bless my husband with kindness, softness, understanding, and gentleness. Instead of being frustrated with my children's obstinacy, I could pray the blessing of wisdom, temperance, understanding, and self-control over them. My own sinful first thoughts became the very things that led me back around to pursue the fruit of the Spirit.

Then something really revolutionary began to happen. It occurred to me to apply the same principle to myself. In struggling with anger, I would ask the Lord to remove it and instead give me joy, kindness, gentleness, and patience. When I felt like a failure, I'd ask Him to breathe into my heart that He calls me "successful, purposed, triumphant, and a conqueror." My specific identity in Christ became something I could actually start to figure out and access by myself. My own issues became starting points for my own healing.

I began to use my synonyms and antonyms as jumping-off points for Scripture study too. With fear of failure, for example, I started looking up Bible verses about the opposite. Before I knew it, I began to be reminded that God says things like "In all these things we are more than conquerors through him who loved us." And I remembered that "neither death nor life, nor angels nor rulers, nor things present nor things to come, nor powers, nor height nor depth, nor anything else in all creation, will be able to separate us from the love of God in Christ Jesus" (Rom. 8:37–39).

When I'm afraid, I can ask the Lord for opposites, such as courage and strength. When I look up scriptures about fear, courage, and strength, I'm reminded that God says, "There is no fear in love, but perfect love casts out fear. For fear has to do with punishment, and whoever fears has not been perfected in love" (1 John 4:18).

I know that "the LORD is my strength and my shield; in him my heart trusts, and I am helped" (Ps. 28:7).

God tells me, "Be strong and courageous. Do not be frightened, and do not be dismayed, for the LORD your God is with you wherever you go" (Josh. 1:9).

A natural part of a believer's identity is curiosity. We want to know more about God and more about ourselves. It's what drives us in pursuit of Him, in pursuit of what He has for our lives. But if we lose ourselves, we'll naturally lose our curiosity for what God could have for our lives as well. We won't trust Him, because at the end of the day, we're deciding that what He says about us isn't true. When all we feel is lost and we don't know how to get out of the woods, we just have to start remembering what it is to be found. We have to remind ourselves who God says we are.

Look up the verses that correspond with your struggles and the fruit you're pursuing. Write them on Post-it notes. Put them on your mirror, your cabinets, or your lower back. (Wait … maybe not the last one!) Really, though, God gives us His Word to pull us out of the muck. Write it down so you can write it on your heart. Memorize the heck out of some scriptures that remind you of who you are. I promise that on your worst day, or even on a mediocre one, *you will forget*. Take what the enemy means to harm you and turn it into the tool to strengthen your faith. What was once your sin can now be the coals that simply stoke the Refiner's fire.

Instead of allowing lies and insecurities to tell me who I am, I ask God to show me what He says about me. And when I forget— which, for crying out loud, is easy to do in this broken world—I just break out my synonym and antonym finder alongside a Bible word search and go to town reminding myself who God says I am.

Pursuit indicates forward movement. And when you're stuck, you just need to go back to the basics to get moving again.

God is good and He is for you, and the things He says about you are true!

Chapter 4

The Illusion of Control

I want the world. I want the whole world. I want to lock it all
up in my pocket. It's my bar of chocolate. Give it to me now!
Veruca Salt, from *Willy Wonka and the Chocolate Factory*

Family movie night is a thing in our house. We all snuggle together in bed, make a huge bowl of popcorn that inevitably leaves trace amounts of kernels that stab me in the night, and settle in to enjoy a movie together. As our boys have gotten older, Jeremy and I have had fun introducing them to some of our favorite childhood flicks: *Star Wars, The Swiss Family Robinson, Pippi Longstocking*, and my personal all-time favorite *Willy Wonka and the Chocolate Factory*.

I love how rewatching movies as an adult gives me such a different perspective from the things I noticed as a kid. When I finally was able to share *Willy Wonka* with the boys, the film hit me in ways that began to reshape my views of God and myself. (If you haven't seen the movie, really, you must. But please watch the older version with Gene Wilder; it's far less creepy than the newer one with Johnny Depp![1])

Willy Wonka, master of glorious confectionary inventions, had dreams, plans, and ideas beyond anything that anyone had imagined before. Locked behind great iron gates in his factory were wonders inconceivable. No one had ever entered Wonka's factory, but it was generally understood that much goodness was contained within the walls. The innovation and creativity of the delicious candies that emerged were proof enough that the man behind it all had greater vision that any other candy maker in the world. There was no doubt in anyone's mind that Wonka was a creative genius, known all over the world for the goodness he produced.

As the story goes, Wonka ran a contest to give five lucky children access to his mysterious factory of candy-making wonder. The whole globe became a frenzy of candy buyers, each trying to find a golden ticket hidden in a chocolate bar to secure his or her place in this once-in-a-lifetime opportunity. One at a time, odds reduced as children around the world scrambled to find tickets. Finally all five were discovered, and the day came when the whole world watched as the children and their guardians entered the magnificent world of Willy Wonka.

Once inside, the children began to tour the fantastical facility. One by one, each child made choices along the journey that disqualified him or her from continuing the experience. I watched Mike Teavee's ironic obsession with technology keep him from advancing farther into Willy Wonka's wonderland. Augustus Gloop's gluttonous idolatry led to his eventual demise. Violet Beauregarde's impatience to enjoy something not yet ready to be experienced kept her from enjoying future opportunities. Veruca Salt's desire to control everything around her made her intolerable and ousted her from the adventure too. It was Charlie Bucket, the child who remained humble and curious, who eventually won the keys to the entire factory. (*Spoiler alert … sorry about that!)

If there's one thing life keeps teaching me, it's that I can't actually control the journey despite my best attempts. And God in His goodness continues to show me that if I'll just quit trying, He can take me places I've never even dared to imagine. Where once I saw a handful of kids entering the candy factory of a great confectionary genius, I now imagine my own humanity staring down the kingdom of God. In Mike, Veruca, Violet, Augustus, and Charlie, I recognize pieces of myself that could set me wandering outside of the goodness meant for me, or that could hand me the keys to access it all.

The night we watched *Willy Wonka*, I saw so much of myself in each of these children and began to ponder all the ways that I, too, disrupt the goodness God has for me. I saw impatience, selfishness, gluttony even for good things, and idolatry standing in the way of following God into His goodness with reckless abandon. The truth of the matter is that this very realization is what set me on the path of pursuing curiosity for God and even writing this book. As I looked at Charlie Bucket, I saw a child born into poverty and brokenness who longed to see and experience the fullness of the great inventor, Willy Wonka, and his inconceivable goodness. I realized that it was Charlie's humility, his trust in the creator, and his curiosity to see more of what was possible that kept him in the adventure. His curious and continuous pursuit of what he knew to be good opened the doors for him to experience all the possibility beyond what he could have imagined for himself.

I realized that if I wanted to truly inherit the kingdom of God, I needed to let go of all I try to control and learn to do the same thing.

THE GENESIS OF CONTROL

According to Genesis, it seems that humanity may have had some control issues from the very beginning. We have ideas about what we want and what we think is best, and we allow those ideas to define our actions. We believe it's to our benefit to make our own choices … to chart our own paths. When Adam and Eve were faced with a life-and-death choice, they listened to the wrong advice:

> The serpent said to the woman, "You will not surely die. For God knows that when you eat of [the fruit] your eyes will be opened, and you will be like God, knowing good and evil." So when the woman saw that the tree was good for food, and that it was a delight to the eyes, and that the tree was to be desired to make one wise, she took of its fruit and ate, and she also gave some to her husband who was with her, and he ate….
>
> Then the LORD God said, "Behold, the man has become like one of us in knowing good and evil. Now, lest he reach out his hand and take also of the tree of life and eat, and live forever—" therefore the LORD God sent him out from the garden of Eden to work the ground from which he was taken. (3:4–6, 22–23)

Bet that's not what Adam and Eve were expecting. They tried to increase their understanding and, in doing so, became aware of brokenness and pain and good and evil. God intended to keep their understanding simple and pure. Since they thought they knew better than God, their eyes were opened to brokenness that the Lord wanted to spare them from experiencing. We wonder why bad things happen to good people, but the thing is that we were never supposed to know the difference in the first place.

We want to control the way things go in our lives. We want to plan and to have things go according to our plans. But so often, if we're honest, they just don't. And really, they can't. Because when we live with a holy God in the midst of a broken world, we just can't control the way it all goes. The world itself is at odds. Good and evil clash, and because of the attempts Adam and Eve made to secure their own understanding, we now all live with the knowledge of that clash. And no matter how hard we try, we aren't the moderators of the battle that rages around us.

Control is defined as "the power to influence or direct people's behavior or the course of events."[2] We assume that if we can produce our own results, the outcomes will be to our satisfaction. If we can direct the events of our lives, then surely the dreams and plans we have for our lives will be the best and will result in happiness. In trying to control our own outcomes, we assume that we must know what's best for our lives. On some level I think we are spiritually arrogant. As if we're the all-knowing and all-seeing One who spoke the heavens into orbit and covered the moon with but a breath.

Can you imagine what it must have been like to be Job? An entire book of the Bible was written about a man who knew better than anyone what it was to live a life outside of his own control. His laments and conversations with friends about his torment span thirty-seven heartbreaking chapters. And in chapter 38, the Lord finally answered Job. I can't even imagine how Job felt when the God of creation spoke to him "out of the whirlwind" and said,

> Who is this that darkens counsel by words
> > without knowledge?
> Dress for action like a man;
> > I will question you, and you make it
> > > known to me.

> Where were you when I laid the foundation of
> > the earth?
> > Tell me, if you have understanding.
> Who determined its measurements—surely
> > you know! (vv. 1–5)

As I read the Lord's correction, I feel a crawl-under-a-rock kind of shame in my own arrogant heart. As if I know what is best. As. If.

I don't know about you, but I figure that if I'm picking what is good for my life, then it's all going to feel good, look good, taste good, smell good, and be visibly good to anyone who sees it. But the truth is, if I'm honest with myself, even some of the things that have looked "bad" from the outside have turned out to be good for me. Hard things make us dig deep within ourselves to find strength we didn't know we had. Loss can teach us to appreciate the blessings that surround us. And while I don't want to minimize the depth of any pain and the *years* it can take for many of us to overcome the brokenness we experience in this life, there is good to be found, even in the hard and even through the bad.

In the ache I still feel over my lost children, I've found a new understanding and compassion for other women that I'd never have known had I not understood the pain of this loss myself. In learning to wait for things I wanted and wasn't getting (or still haven't seen come to fruition), I've developed patience and grace. In experiencing pain at the hands of hurt people, I've learned that hurt people hurt people. When I've walked through things that don't look good or feel good, I've found new grace and healing in the brokenness. And while hurt people may hurt people, healed people heal people.

Maybe sometimes we do think we can control the way things go. I mean, to some extent we have the capacity to define our own paths. We can make decisions that shape the way we live. If we eat healthy food, our bodies will function better. When we exercise, our muscles grow stronger and increase our physical capacity. By avoiding dangerous behaviors, we can reduce the incidence of injury. To some extent we can direct behaviors and events, but when we allow that thinking to rule the way we live, we also lose the capacity to be curious about things unknown and outside of our own plans, outside of our limited view.

As Lovelle Drachman once said, "Blessed are the curious … for they shall have adventures." But we can't be curious about something we control. And, friend, when we try to control our lives, we miss out on the adventure of faith. If we always see or know where we're going or what we're doing, we'll miss Wonkaland. We will miss the kingdom of God.

THE MOCKING VAN

When I got pregnant with my first child, it was pretty much a cakewalk. Only three months into trying, I turned up pregnant lickety-split when my husband winked at me real good one day. I craved Mexican food like it was my job, gained the recommended amount of weight, cut out coffee and fish containing mercury, and was pretty much a happy little pregnant person whose nose never even spread wide across my face. Lucky me.

I figured it'd always be the same after that. Easy-peasy lemon-squeezey pregnancies for me. Naturally my husband and I needed to make room for our perfectly expanding little dream.

I'm only five foot four. This matters because it means that pretty much every vehicle ever made will fit me. I can scoot the driver's seat as far forward as I need to, and my head will never hit the sunroof. I'm a great fit for most standard vehicles, and despite being relatively short, I'm still tall enough to see just fine over most any steering wheel. I'm an ideal car-buying customer: my options are endless.

But my husband … not so much. He, on the other hand, is six foot six. He's part of the reason, okay *the* reason, we sold the cute little convertible I had when we got married. I loved everything about that car, but his head hit the roof when he drove it. Also, he could never get the seat to go back quite far enough to keep his knees from pressing a bit into the dash.

So we sold my convertible and eventually got a gently-used Honda Pilot SUV. It got pretty decent gas mileage, was comfortable to drive, would fit our dogs in the back, and didn't cost us an arm and a leg. Plus, my husband's arms and legs fit comfortably, which was sort of a requirement. It accommodated Walker's car seat just fine behind the passenger seat and seemed like it would be a great family car for years to come. That is, until I got pregnant when my man winked at me a second time, and we realized we'd have two children in car seats simultaneously. We couldn't all fit with a car seat behind the driver's side.

So we decided to get a new car.

Armed with two car seats and some research, we decided to take the plunge and get a minivan. Most of the bones in my body screamed at me for the decision to basically succumb to donning the mom jeans of the automobile world. But the side door that opened with the push of a button on a rainy day was just too much to resist. Plus, we could actually fit *four* car seats in the van no matter who was driving.

I'm the negotiator in our family, so on October 31, 2007, I sold our Honda Pilot to a really darling husband and wife and had them drop me off at the car dealership to buy a new van. Three months pregnant and armed with resolve and a cashier's check for the amount Jeremy and I had decided to pay for the new van, I hopped out at the Honda dealership to find the Odyssey minivan of my childbearing dreams. If they wouldn't sell me a minivan for what we wanted to pay for it, I was going to phone a friend to come pick me up all pregnant and weepy at the entrance of the dealership.

My negotiating plan worked, and at 5:30 p.m. that day, I got a sweet deal on a brand-new minivan. It was my first new car ever, and I drove off the lot with all the happy feelings about the masses of glorious space we had just created for our growing family.

The next morning I hopped into my van, inhaled the smell of brand new, and excitedly drove the mile and a half to my twelve-week maternity checkup.

That was the day the ultrasound-screen heartbeat wasn't blinking. Less than twelve hours after buying our brand-new van, I learned I wouldn't be needing all that extra space after all.

I hated that minivan from the moment I walked out of the doctor's office that day. And as my husband and I struggled for the next several years with infertility and the subsequent loss of multiple pregnancies, I felt like that dang van mocked me. It was a reminder that nothing happened the way I'd planned it. It represented the day we lost our first baby and how everything can change in an instant. The minivan seemed to thumb its nose in my face as I drove one lone child around for more than three years. People who didn't know the situation would tease me about my mom-jeans minivan. Because, let's be honest, pretty much no one gets a minivan for just one kid.

Despite the zillion ways that minivan mocked me, I resolved to enjoy the automated sliding door in the rain as much as I possibly could. I'd put Walker in through the side, and then I'd get in there too and crawl into the front seat. You know, so I could be dry while I buckled him in with all that extra space around me. I'd be darned if I'd let that van destroy me! After all, it was just a car, and I knew that my God was bigger than even a mocking minivan.

What in your life is mocking you? What's the salt in your wounds that you wake up to nearly every day? What have you set in motion that thumbs its nose at you over and over? You can't control it and are stuck with it for a while. So what are you gonna do? Are you letting it rule you?

I'm not suggesting that you shouldn't just change things up if you have the chance. But in the meantime, can you rise above the issue? Can you believe that there is more for you? Can you accept that there can still be something good to find even inside a minivan part of life that seems to turn your dreams into a joke? I know it's hard. I'm with you. But when you can't control the circumstances, the only thing you can change is if or how you allow them to control you.

I'm happy to say that after driving it for almost eight years, we finally sold the minivan. I let go of the long season of dreams that it had always held for me. I let go of the control that I never had in the first place. Even better, we got a new-to-us car. With our two boys, who had left an entire bench seat empty in the back of the van for years, my husband and I went together and bought a ten-year-old four-seat convertible. While the family we are isn't the family I thought we'd be, we're embracing our present beautiful reality and looking forward with curiosity to all the roads we have yet to travel in pursuit of possibilities we have yet to imagine.

And we're doing it with the top down....

RAT RACES AND RABBIT TRAILS

I read one time in an ultimate survival guide that if you're ever chased by an alligator, you should run really fast, zigzagging back and forth to confuse the gator and slow it down so it doesn't catch you and bite you in half. You're welcome for that little lifesaving nugget. Should you ever find yourself in a swamp, you can remember that and save your life. Or if you live in Florida or Louisiana, just consider it a refresher of what you already knew. Anyhow ... I digress.

The point I have yet to make is that I think life probably looks a whole lot more like a zigzag trail than a straight shot on an interstate highway to get where you're trying to go—whether you're being chased by an alligator or not.

I like to think of life with God sort of like following along a rabbit trail. I'm not a Native American tracker with wilderness expertise or anything, but I have watched little Peter Cottontail go hopping down a bunny trail in the woods before. And to even an inexperienced animal tracker like me, those little trails look as if the bunny may have been chased by an alligator. The trails zig this way and then zag back the other way. They go over some logs and under others. It doesn't seem most of the time like there's a whole lot of rhyme or reason to where those trails are going, but my understanding is that the ultimate goal is to end up in a safe little burrow called home.

Control is an illusion, and complete understanding is beyond our capacity. I think that most of the time, life is actually a series of redirections and detours. In the end, if we're all going to end up at home, why do we feel the pressure to always get there the same way? Why do we think that the trail has to be marked or that the path must always be straight? By the same token, do we all journey along the same path to faith in Jesus, or does God not lead us to the truth from different directions?

Robert Frost said, "Two roads diverged in a wood, and I— / I took the one less traveled by, / and that has made all the difference."[3]

Why are we so afraid of the "road less traveled"—the road we don't know? Our desire to control the way so often impedes our ability to experience new journeys.

Do you always take the same route home? Or do you switch it up? Are you so afraid of getting lost, or taking longer to get where you're going, that you're unwilling to see what could be in store for you along the way? I wonder how often we get stuck in the same ruts because of our unwillingness to trust God enough to walk into the unknown. How often does our need to control rob us of delights that God desires us to experience? I bet a whole lot of the time we miss out on seeing ways in which He longs to shepherd us as we explore life.

Why don't we trust God and what His Word says about Him?

> You [God] make known to me the path of life;
> in your presence there is fullness of joy;
> at your right hand are pleasures
> forevermore. (Ps. 16:11)

> He leads the humble in what is right,
> and teaches the humble his way.
> All the paths of the LORD are steadfast love
> and faithfulness,
> for those who keep his covenant and his
> testimonies. (Ps. 25:9–10)

On the other hand, a whole lot of the time, instead of zigging and zagging to explore new pathways, we get caught up in what feels like a rat race. One minute we may be fine meandering this way and that in life, trusting God at each turn, but then we catch a glimpse of where we think He might be taking us. Suddenly we're hardly following God anymore as we focus on what lies at the end of the journey. We become so obsessed with obtaining what appears to lie within our reach that we veer off the lovely back roads of life, where God wants to reveal a peaceful landscape to us. Before we even know what's happening, we're speeding up an on-ramp to a busy interstate and find ourselves stuck in endless traffic that jams up our purpose and plan. The goal appears to lie ahead, but the journey to get there becomes more about safely navigating the insanity around us than about enjoying the trip. We try to control the journey so we'll get where we're going in the most direct and expedient way, and so often we miss out on the gifts God wants to reveal to us when we zig and zag as we follow Him.

How often do we turn our eyes from following God and instead follow other people? Instead of journeying the road God has for us, we focus on someone else's destination and find ourselves on a pathway we were never meant to travel. Scripture tells us,

> A man's ways are before the eyes of the LORD,
>   and he ponders all his paths.
> The iniquities of the wicked ensnare him,
>   and he is held fast in the cords of his sin.
> He dies for lack of discipline,
>   and because of his great folly he is led
>   astray. (Prov. 5:21–23)

Maybe the greatest way that God could ever lead us is by the road less traveled. It's a rabbit trail that to our unbelieving eyes looks like a desert road leading to a vast sea with no discernible way across. Yet God carves out a path ahead of us, just as He did for the Israelites:

> Your way was through the sea,
>   your path through the great waters;
>   yet your footprints were unseen.

> You led your people like a flock
> by the hand of Moses and Aaron.
> (Ps. 77:19–20)

What if the greatest story of your life is waiting to happen on a zigzag outside of your control? Are you curious enough to follow? Do you trust God enough to believe that the road He leads you on won't end where sand meets water, but that He'll make a way where there wouldn't have been one without Him?

The more we try to control, the less we can let go and trust the vision of our Creator. And if we choose to live in an illusion or can't adjust our expectations, we'll often be disappointed and miss out on the fullness that can be ours when we choose to curiously pursue God.

Years ago Nationwide insurance had a catchy slogan that said, "Life comes at you fast." The circumstances of our lives and the feelings that surround them can become roadblocks that cripple our walk with God. In the chapters that follow, we'll dig into some of the inhibitors of a curious faith and learn how to overcome them. We'll start slow with issues like worry and fear before we find ourselves on our faces before God in the midst of our broken and messy lives. It's a journey, friend, and we don't go it alone. Hold my hand, and let's walk together.

PART 2

Anything but Curious

Chapter 5

Reexamining Wilderness

*To be commanded to love God at all, let alone in the wilderness, is
like being commanded to be well when we are sick, to sing for joy
when we are dying of thirst, to run when our legs are broken. But
this is the first and great commandment nonetheless. Even in the
wilderness—especially in the wilderness—you shall love him.*

Frederick Buechner, *A Room Called Remember*

"I guess I just want to thank you for all the years of growth I've
experienced here," I said through teary eyes. "But it just seems like
our time here is done."

My husband and I sat in the church office, facing the founding
pastor as I recounted to him the years of my life there. I had been
involved in women's ministry, taught elementary-age Sunday school
classes, discipled high school youth, and spearheaded a remodel project to turn the old sanctuary into a modern youth building. For the
past eight months, I had been a fixture in the church building, working on various projects four times per week, and the previous week,

I'd decorated the sanctuary for Christmas. Most of my friendships had been made through the ministries I was involved in, and over the course of eleven years, this church had become a second home to me. My life was wrapped up between the walls beneath that steeple.

I had never left a church before, particularly not one that held so many people I loved and deeply respected. Jeremy and I couldn't ignore it, though; we just didn't feel like we fit anymore. We had reached a point where it seemed that the best thing for everyone was for us to leave as well as we possibly could. So we extended thanks and blessing and didn't bother asking the questions whose answers wouldn't have made any difference.

My husband sat quietly through most of the meeting. He had already met with another executive pastor several times to make sure we understood fully the things we were questioning. He had said his piece, but I needed closure, so we scheduled this meeting for me to find some. I needed to be heard. I needed to say "thank you" and "I'm sad to leave."

"Where do you think you'll go?" the pastor asked us matter-of-factly.

I shrugged my shoulders and turned to face my husband. Perhaps he would know what to say. The truth was that we had no idea where we were going next. Our future felt very nebulous.

"To the wilderness," my husband said. "We're going to the wilderness."

And that is exactly where we went.

For the next several months, we felt as if we were wandering. My heart was still broken into a million tiny pieces from losing our baby. Add to that dose of depression a significant loss of community, and I found myself very much alone. People at church were offended by our decision to leave, and relationships fractured in the tension. Jeremy and I tried a few different churches and even settled into a small start-up for a few months, but most weeks I could barely hold myself together through an entire service. My husband's job was a source of stress and frustration, and it felt as if all the pieces of our lives were falling apart. For months I didn't know who I was, and I didn't have anywhere to belong. I thought I'd die in that wilderness.

FEELING FORGOTTEN

Wilderness doesn't always have to be a lonely and barren season. Sometimes it can be as simple as longing for something seemingly far away. We all have dreams of adventure and new experiences. We imagine components of our lives with different endings. What choices could have led us down different roads from the ones we may walk even now? Wilderness isn't always desolation. Sometimes it just feels as if we're forgotten. There is a sadness in unmet longing, but if we aren't careful, those seemingly innocent unmet longings can land us squarely in the wilderness. We may find ourselves in seasons of disappointment and hopelessness if we choose to focus on unmet hopes and expectations instead of looking for the blessings of today. Isn't disappointment just a part of living? Yet we want to keep it from influencing our capacity to walk in hope and curiosity.

Jeremy and I inherited a wide-planked double swing when we moved into our home. The huge old oak tree in our front yard has a perfect branch that the previous owners made excellent use of when they installed the swing. I've been surprised at how frequently we go outside and play on that swing.

"Mommy, come swing with us," my children beckon to me.

"Push us higher, Daddy!" they squeal as we soar up into the air together.

The delight our family has experienced with the swing not only has provided a sweet time of connection for us but also has been a gateway to building friendships with neighbors walking by. Some of my greatest memories in our home have come from a couple of lengths of rope and an extralong plank of pine hanging from a big old tree in the yard.

What if some of the very best gifts are just thirty steps from your front door? The goodness of God is all around you because the Giver loves to delight His children. The question is, in seasons of plenty or of wilderness, are you willing to look around to find that goodness? Are you curious about the gifts of today that can help move you through a season when you feel forgotten?

Perhaps part of learning to really live and embrace the life you've been given is to be present in the now. Maybe it means saying no to what seem like adventures because you know your family isn't in a season where it can handle change well. Perhaps finances and time are preventing you from achieving dreams you've had since you were young.

Life just doesn't work out the way we so often dream and hope it will. I'd guess that twenty years from now, even if we fully satisfy our longings, there will be things we'll wish we'd done differently.

When our longings are unmet, we must learn to embrace a more eternal perspective. If we can't learn to see the goodness of life in seasons of unmet longing, we won't know how to find it when we're in a blatantly desolate wilderness either. The apostle Paul reminds us that God's goodness is rooted in eternity, not in earthly things:

> We do not lose heart. Though our outer self is wasting away, our inner self is being renewed day by day. For this light momentary affliction is preparing for us an eternal weight of glory beyond all comparison, as we look not to the things that are seen but to the things that are unseen. For the things that are seen are transient, but the things that are unseen are eternal. (2 Cor. 4:16–18)

King Solomon was among the wealthiest and wisest men who ever lived. His life was full of lavish excess. He had seven hundred wives, incomparable riches, and wisdom seemingly unmatched even thousands of years later. Yet he said, "I have seen everything that is done under the sun, and behold, all is vanity and a striving after wind" (Eccles. 1:14).

If our longings were met, I wonder if we'd even know it. If we can't learn to find life and hope in seasons of unmet longing, then pieces of us will likely still feel dead even when we should be content. God may eventually satisfy our desires in ways we imagine, or in His goodness He may rewrite them altogether.

PRECONCEIVED RESENTMENTS

When I was in college, I'll never forget my friend Trisha once saying, "Expectations are preconceived resentments." I think we were talking about something relatively unimportant when she dropped that little nugget into the middle of a thought. But that nugget stuck with me for a long time.

I had to think for a while about the possibility that our expectations are actually preconceived resentments. It's true, because so often when things don't go the way we want or expect, we get upset. We have an idea about what we want or where we're going, and when that doesn't come to pass, we feel disappointed, discouraged, or maybe even rejected or angry.

Paramount maturity, right?

I see it in my children all the time. Maybe they wake up one morning and remember the candy my mom gave them the week before. They rise early, thoughts lingering on the sweetness experienced before, and suddenly they expect to experience it again, *immediately*. It must happen now in alignment with their present desires. At 7:00 a.m., they announce to me, full of assurance and expectation, "Mommy, we're going to eat our candy now."

"Um … no. We're not going to eat candy right now," I tell them. "We just woke up. You may have fruit or yogurt instead. You can have your candy after lunch."

Wails ensue that the neighbors can hear, and suddenly what began as an unmet expectation turns into an all-out battle of wills and subsequent discipline for ridiculous fits of rage thrown in opposition to my decision.

Expectations become preconceived resentments. When expectations are left unmet, they can incite anger, frustration, fear, and even willful disobedience. And from there, we walk right into a wilderness of our own making.

Over the years, though, I see the ways this crops up in my own life. I get an idea that a plan I have will go a certain way. But when things don't work out the way I plan and expect, I end up frustrated, upset, mad, sad, whatever.

Maybe you planned to get married right out of college because it's what your parents did. Now it's spring term senior year, and you haven't so much as gone on a single date with anyone. Shoot! What now? Maybe you expected that the job you landed would lead you up the corporate ladder into glowing success. Perhaps the family you've been planning since getting your first Cabbage Patch doll was supposed to come easy. Then hello, miscarriage and infertility. Enter a lengthy bout with depression and a bad attitude. *Why me, God? Things aren't exactly going according to plan here, and I'm ticked.*

Many of the things we hope for are story lines we've planned out for our lives, sometimes intentionally and sometimes inadvertently. We see things in our mind's eye, imagine what we're hoping for, set our sights on goals and ideas of what we believe will be good for us. We place those goals, desires, dreams, and aspirations at the end of a hopeful road and hold fast to a passport for that expected destination.

But when our expectations for this life don't turn out as imagined, we take offense and become resentful toward God. We recall past disappointments and determine that maybe God doesn't want what's good for us after all. We forget His bigness and goodness, as well as the possibility He has for us. The memories of past hardships in life come rushing back to assure us that this place, where what we wanted doesn't come to pass, is the place we're meant to be.

Instead of believing that God is good and is for us, we begin to believe that perhaps God is a harsh disciplinarian who is punishing us or teaching us a lesson. The distrust and broken hope we're left holding in our hands lead us to believe that we're out of favor with God. We may spend years wandering around in a place we don't know and never wanted to be. And God is just a big, fat jerk.

Welcome to the wilderness … where you feel alone, forgotten, hopeless, and angry.

DON'T WASTE YOUR WILDERNESS

The story of a slave woman named Hagar is one of the first places wilderness is mentioned in the Bible. God had promised to make nations through Abraham and his barren wife, Sarah. But rather than trusting God, they took matters into their own hands and decided that an extramarital affair was the solution to their infertility problems. So Abe shacked up with Sarah's slave to bear offspring. After a son, Ishmael, was born to Hagar, Sarah sent them away. Because, seriously, what wife ever thinks it's a great idea to keep a mistress around? Yeah, I'm with you, sister. *Absolutely not!*

Genesis 21:14 says of Hagar, "She departed and wandered in the wilderness of Beersheba." And so Hagar, Sarah's slave, was used up and abandoned because she followed her mistress's orders. I'm just gonna guess that Hagar left with a whole lot of unmet expectations. Cast into a wasteland of desolation, she believed that she and the child would die when their food and water ran out. Geez … can you even imagine?

In the book of Numbers, we see Moses and Aaron deliver the Israelites from slavery in Egypt. The journey from there to the Promised Land was about 240 miles and should have taken them only about two weeks. Instead, the Israelites made some poor choices that left them wandering in the wilderness for forty years. A two-week journey turned into *forty years* of wilderness. Ugh ... depressing.

The shepherd boy David had a kingly anointing on his life. But when a jealous King Saul threatened to kill him, David fled to the wilderness and hid in caves. Fearing for his life as his enemies pursued him for nearly four years, David was forced into the wilderness. The wilderness was the only place he could go to escape death.

In the wilderness, David wrote, "O God, you are my God; earnestly I seek you; my soul thirsts for you; my flesh faints for you, as in a dry and weary land where there is no water" (Ps. 63:1).

Life in the wilderness sure can take a toll on a soul.

Over and over in the Old Testament, it seems that people were driven into the wilderness. Despite my sadness for the isolation these people must have felt, I can't help but notice the ever-presence of a loving God, even in those places of desolation.

Genesis tells us that the Lord sent an angel to encourage Hagar in the wilderness. He provided a well in the middle of nowhere when her water ran out, and he remained with Hagar and her son during that long season of wilderness. Later on, Ishmael became an expert bowman, and through him the Lord kept His promise to Hagar and brought forth the Arab nations.

No one knows longing like the Israelites, who lived for years in anticipation of the land flowing with milk and honey that God had promised them. They wandered in the wilds of vast lands before crossing into the Promised Land, and yet there was goodness even in their wandering. Even in their longing for more, even in the wilderness, there was enough for each day.

For the Israelites, the Red Sea parted and made way for the people to cross over to the Promised Land. Despite the Israelites' disobedience and grumbling in the wilderness, a pillar of cloud in the sky led them by day, and a pillar of fire illuminated the way at night. The presence of the Lord hovered over them as they wandered. Manna fell from heaven to feed them, satisfying the exact amount of food they needed each day—no more, no less. The Lord planned for them to take over the Promised Land. But instead of choosing to believe that what God had for them was good, they disobeyed and landed themselves in punishment for forty years. Refusal to walk into what God had purposed kept them in a place of wandering for a good long while, but the presence of the Lord remained steady.

The Lord protected David in his season of wilderness as well. First Samuel tells us that "David remained in the strongholds in the wilderness, in the hill country of the wilderness of Ziph. And Saul sought him every day, but God did not give him into his hand" (23:14). Though David wandered and spent a long season in hiding, the Lord covered and sustained him during those years.

As I've struggled with my own expectations and lost hope, I've realized that the new covenant of Christ offers a fresh perspective of wilderness. In the Old Testament, the wilderness was often a place where people were sent for punishment or, in David's case, fled to escape death, but the New Testament frames it in a different light.

John the Baptist spent most of his life in the wilderness. The time he spent there prepared him to proclaim the coming of the Lord. The wilderness training was what made John able to fulfill the role God called him to play. John was wild and rugged and lived with abandon. He knew the things he was called to and didn't allow outside pressures to distract him from his calling. His faithfulness became known everywhere, and people even began to seek him out in the wilderness. Arriving with repentant hearts, those who sought out the dry lands, where life's pretense fades away, came to experience renewal. It was in the wilderness that they experienced baptism. John the Baptist met people in the wilderness, and they emerged with fresh hope and new life.

Jesus Himself spent forty days in the wilderness. Tempted by satan, He went without food and water for more than a month! And let's not forget that it was the Holy Spirit who actually led Him there to be tested. When Jesus was finally brought to the end of Himself, the Bible says that the devil left Him, and angels came and ministered to Him. Emerging from the season of testing, He launched His public ministry. Without the wilderness, even Jesus wouldn't have been prepared for the mission God had for Him.

By the time we get to the apostle Paul, he was choosing to enter the wilderness himself. He recognized the need to shed the patterns of the world to transform his mind. The wilderness stripped away pretense and created a clear space for him to hear the Lord speak.

When we look back again to the Psalms, David talked about the wilderness and I think perhaps figured out a few things we could stand to learn. Interestingly enough, the Lord has given me this passage for several people when they've walked through difficult seasons, when disappointments have set in and hope seems to have fled:

> You crown the year with your bounty;
> your wagon tracks overflow with
> abundance.
> The pastures of the wilderness overflow,
> the hills gird themselves with joy.
> (Ps. 65:11–12)

Hidden among hills to save his life, David found that even when we're tucked out of view, sent away from home, and wandering to stay alive, we can find joy. In fact, the pastures of the wilderness *overflow* with joy! In seasons where life seems stripped down and barren, we can do more than just survive. We can receive abundance!

Perhaps we've landed in the wilderness because of disobedience. Or maybe like the Israelites, we refused to believe that the goodness God gives is truly ours to receive. When we're facing disappointment, unmet expectations, or even seasons of prolonged wilderness wanderings, could it be that what the Lord has for us is training? In the wilderness, when we're lost and discouraged and can't find our way home, the only thing we're supposed to find is the Way. In the place we're lost, can we realize it's there that we're found? In the wilderness, when all else is gone, can we find fresh curiosity for God? In our isolation, can we have renewed hope in all that God has for us?

One gift of the wilderness is the clarity we gain when all else is stripped away. When life feels bare, it's easier to see what is truly important. Priorities align, distractions fade away, and we find ourselves in an environment where we can dig deeper into our faith.

Imagine yourself standing in a desert. Sand for miles, heat rising in nearly visible waves that hover above the ground. Golden earth meets blue sky, and nothing interrupts the view of a vast wasteland. But then a figure appears. You blink to make sure you see correctly. Sure enough, a man walks toward you. With nothing else obstructing the view, you can clearly see the person of God in front of you. Suddenly wilderness isn't so isolated when God is there with you.

In many biblical situations, God revealed Himself most clearly to His people in the wilderness, like Moses, Hagar, Elijah, David, John the Baptist, Saul, and Jesus. Over and over, the Spirit of the Lord appeared to His people in the desert, ministering to them and training them in their unique seasons of wilderness.

What if we begin to see the wilderness as a training ground? As a sharpening iron? As a space to find clarity and purpose?

I don't doubt that your wilderness, like mine, may be a hot mess of disaster straight from the pit of hell. The devil will try anything to absolutely level you and your faith. But our enemy doesn't want your life. He doesn't want your job or your family or your happiness. Instead, he wants to rob you of your faith. He wants to weaken the army of God here on this earth by taking you out of it. So my question to you is, when the devil holds you down and threatens your life in the wilderness, will you just give up and hand your faith to him? Will you believe his lies about your identity and let him rob you of hope for the future?

If you have the power of Jesus Christ in you—which, for the record, you have when you accept His sacrifice as payment for your life—then no enemy can defeat you. Satan can try to destroy you. He can mess up your life just as he did with Job. But, friend, I want to challenge you and to challenge myself. If satan is messing with you, it's because he's worried about you. You carry a great and powerful Jesus in you ... the same One who rose from the grave and defeated death. The Jesus who redeems and restores and *always* wins. No matter what it is that lands you in a wilderness—whether you're there for discipline, or the enemy has pushed you there, or you walk into it yourself—you *must* know that you can emerge sharper, more victorious, more full of hope, and with a renewed curiosity for God. Our buddy Paul knew a thing or two about this when he wrote,

> We are afflicted in every way, but not crushed; perplexed, but not driven to despair; persecuted, but not forsaken; struck down, but not destroyed; always carrying in the body the death of Jesus, *so that the life of Jesus may also be manifested in our bodies.* For we who live are always being given over to death for Jesus' sake, so that the life of Jesus also may be manifested in our mortal flesh. So death is at work in us, but life in you. (2 Cor. 4:8–12)

Maybe it's the fighter in me. Or perhaps it's the perseverance my dad taught me from a young age. You don't give up. You don't give in. You finish what you've begun. Don't sign up if you're not willing to show up. Being a finisher exhibits integrity ... an ability to stick with things. You do what you say, and you mean what you do. You finish what you start and do your darnedest to do it well. Though a wilderness may threaten to crush you, you will not be destroyed!

Isaiah 43:19 says,

> Behold, I am doing a new thing;
> now it springs forth, do you not perceive it?
> I will make a way in the wilderness
> and rivers in the desert.

God will make a way for you in the wilderness. You can find fields of joy, sustenance for today, hope for the future, and the renewal of baptism in the wilderness if you're willing to open your eyes to see them.

Wilderness is an opportunity for rootedness in Christ. Can we begin to see it that way? Wilderness can be preparation for launching into ministry. Wilderness has the capacity to be a season of renewal and fresh baptism.

So often we allow a season of wilderness to defeat us instead of prepare us to be launched into something new. Are we missing the manna God provides to sustain us for each day? Are we starving because we refuse to gather up the goodness or see the well in the desert? In our unmet longings, do we refuse to look up and see the pillar of the Lord's presence hovering and illuminating the way? How often are we wasting our wilderness experience because we are blind to the clarity that can come when all else is stripped away?

A HALLWAY OF POSSIBILITY

We may think we're in a wilderness, but what if we're actually in a hallway of possibility? Sometimes we're stuck in the wilderness because we stop looking for a way out. We stop looking for possibility. We lose the curiosity to uncover new goodness.

Now, I believe firmly in the God who parts the sea, feeds thousands, and heals the sick laid in front of Him, but so often I think we believe that we'll always inherit goodness at no cost to ourselves. That a promised land is always simple, that it drops in front of us as obviously as manna from heaven.

God is certainly an opener of doors and a creator of opportunity, but He wants us to be curious enough to pursue Him and find the additional gifts He has for us along the way.

There are a handful of Christian sayings I find annoying and even unbiblical. The one I hear frequently that probably gets under my skin the most is "I'm just waiting on the Lord to open the door."

This sounds to me as if we've determined exactly where we're supposed to be going, and we're just waiting on God to open the door that meets our expectations. We find ourselves standing at the end of a road armed with clear expectations of what we believe comes next. It's as if we are waiting for trumpets to blast and gates to be flung wide open before us.

We think God will say, "Welcome, My child, to the land of promise and plenty. Walk on in! I've opened the way before you. No rocky road, no paths unseen. I've thrown wide the doors, and all you have to do is walk through them."

The Canaanites, Amorites, Hittites, Perizzites, and Jebusites didn't throw a party and invite the Israelites to come in and inhabit the Promised Land. God promised the land to them. Caleb and Joshua knew that the Lord was with the Israelites to take over the space, but it would require them to actually fight for what was offered to them.

Sometimes we must be willing to push into the spaces we know God has for us. Perhaps it will require us to move forward with a hope and curiosity that God will just show up again as He has in the past. We may recall a testimony of the Lord's provision that girds our faith to walk into a place that isn't necessarily a clear-cut venture.

For instance, in Mark 2, Jesus healed a paralytic. It's not clear how long the man had been paralyzed, but he came to Jesus to receive healing. The man didn't stay put in his house and wait for Jesus to come running to heal him. He pursued it. He found four friends to take him to see Jesus and hear Him preach. When they couldn't get close enough because of the large crowd, they climbed onto the roof, made a hole, and lowered the man through it. Despite his condition, he believed in the wholeness Jesus offered and continued to chase after the goodness he believed could be for him.

I wonder how often we stand at the end of a road, facing one expected door and waiting for it to open. How often could we actually be in a hallway of possibility? I imagine sometimes that our lives are like a choose-your-own-adventure book.

Possibilities are so varied that we can pick among lots of options. Many times there isn't one clear-cut path. When we're pursuing the Lord, in His kindness, He can bless us many different ways. What if we stop trying to open the same door we have chosen and instead just turn around to see what God has for us? We might realize that, in His goodness, God has placed us in a hallway of unlocked doors of possibility. We could walk down the hallway, jiggling knobs, pushing doors open, and peeking inside to discover new possibilities. We might peer into multiple spaces and hear Him saying to us, "You can stand here in the wilderness of your unmet expectations, or you can enter new lands of possibility that you have yet to dream about."

While walking in the wilderness can certainly feel defeating, perhaps it's meant to be clarifying, sharpening, and reorienting. Wilderness simplifies our way back to God's ways. When we release our own expectations, hope for the future can be reshaped and reimagined. As we release our longings to the Lord and recall the testimony of His goodness and faithfulness to us, our wilderness can become the place that roots us in understanding His heart for us.

It's time we get curious about what God has for us in the wilderness. Are you gonna find out what's in it for you? Because, believe me, something *is* in it for you!

Chapter 6

The DANGER!

Therefore I tell you, do not be anxious about your life, what you
will eat or what you will drink, nor about your body, what you
will put on.... And which of you by being anxious can add a single
hour to his span of life? ... Consider the lilies of the field, how they
grow: they neither toil nor spin, yet I tell you, even Solomon in all
his glory was not arrayed like one of these. But if God so clothes the
grass of the field, which today is alive and tomorrow is thrown into
the oven, will he not much more clothe you, O you of little faith?

Matthew 6:25, 27–30

Strolling along a rambling pathway among vibrantly colored azaleas
and rhododendron, I breathe in the crisp mountain air and feel my
body relax as I take in the scenery around me. I feel exhausted,
overwhelmed, and used up. This hour is meant to help me find
refreshment.

The Biltmore Estate in Asheville, North Carolina, has some
of the most beautifully manicured gardens I've ever seen. Famed

landscape architect Frederick Law Olmsted designed the gardens to feel simultaneously natural and manicured. Smells change along the pathways, with splashes of color and texture all around. I've heard it said that this area of the country is second only to the rain forest for biodiversity.

No matter how many times I walk through Biltmore's lush gardens, I notice completely new plants—different species of shrubs, lilies, and orchids I've not heard of before, and a wide variety of the ever-familiar-to-me azaleas.

An azalea bush beside me bursting with thousands of white blooms hangs partway into the path I'm on. I bend close to examine the flower; five perfectly formed petals with softened edges make a rounded star shape. On the top petal alone, I notice several dozen tiny yellow speckles that look as if they're hand painted. The precision of each tiny dot, so intentionally placed, beckons my curiosity.

"Consider the lilies of the field, how they grow" (Matt. 6:28). My mind lingers on the familiar, old scripture as my eyes focus on the intricacies of the single flower in front of me.

Here I stand in the middle of stunning gardens on a sunny day, practically scrambling for air in the midst of too many things on my plate, and God points out tiny strokes of buttery-yellow specks, hand painted by heaven on milky-white petals.

"Will he not much more clothe you, O you of little faith?" (v. 30).

Repetition drills the concept deeper into my heart as my brain meditates on the thought a few times over. And slowly as I stare and consider the intentionality of the flower bloom in front of me, a bloom that remains for maybe only three weeks before it shrivels and falls to the ground, I begin to feel my tensions ease. As I meditate on the scriptures that tell me to cast off anxiety and worry and peer into the center of a flower no larger than my thumb, I am reminded that my worries only cripple my faith and forward movement.

If we think that life will break us, then at some point we become afraid to really live it. Worry leads us to operate out of fear, forgetting that God paints tiny speckles in the center of small flowers, and in our distrust, we become paralyzed. Worry creates narrow pathways in life, but trusting the One who paints details on flowers opens us to greater perspective and possibility than we have ever imagined.

Fear paralyzes our perspective, but curiosity opens up possibility. Remember, a curious faith is a mobile faith. Worry is just a killjoy. If we allow ourselves to operate from a place of fear, before we know it, fear will define the decisions we make and the steps we take. If we walk in fear, we'll never be willing to step out on a limb because we'll be too afraid it will break. But no one who stays on the ground ever sees the world from the top of the tree. A perspective defined by worry will always be small. We'll never see what could be if we allow fear to define where we go.

Several years ago my aunt gifted my husband and me with a helicopter ride above Glacier National Park in Montana. Jeremy and I spent a few days driving and hiking through the park, enjoying the craggy peaks and lush vistas across fields and lakes. The views took my breath away over and over. But the day we lifted into the sky, hovering above row after row of snowcapped peaks, I felt as if I were in a dream. We flew over lakes, pointed out lookout towers, and crossed the Continental Divide. In one hour my entire perspective of Glacier shifted as we soared above the ground and saw the park from high in the sky. During our ride, though, a storm started to blow in, and low clouds rolled between the peaks. In areas where we should have been able to see for miles, the fog blocked our view.

Worry can be like those clouds, rolling in, obstructing a clear perspective, killing our curiosity. It can actually keep us from pulling out of our lives far enough to get a bird's-eye view in the first place. It's a death trap that will affect the way we make decisions. At the root of worry is fear, and at the root of fear is distrust. So the question becomes, do we trust God or not? Do we trust Him with our finances? Do we trust Him with our children? With our marriages? What about with our hopes and dreams?

As long as we allow worry to define our perspective, we'll always be prisoners to small possibilities. If we allow fear to determine where we go, we'll never see what God could do in our lives. Worry limits possibility because to move forward, we need everything to fall into place or make perfect sense. If we're worried all the time, we won't make a move unless it seems as though all the stars have aligned in our favor. Our worry stunts faith, and faith requires trust. A faith defined by worry is an immobile one. Because gates don't always fling wide open, and the stars of our perfectly laid plans don't always align. God wants us to follow Him whether we can see the path before us or not. We can trust that He will clothe and bless us much more than the flowers He speckles with a detailed brush.

A CRUCIAL TOOTH

One of my favorite T-shirts says, "What doesn't kill you makes you stronger … except bears, because bears will kill you!" And by this point in our journey together, you know I'm a gal who apparently needs to wear the words I want to remember. Besides speaking a nugget of truth, the saying totally makes me laugh.

When I was eight months pregnant with my second child, a childcare worker interrupted me as I was in the middle of a group praying for someone at church one night.

"Um, we have a little bit of a problem, and you may want to come."

I casually walked out of the sanctuary, since the worker's voice hadn't conveyed too much alarm. But as I came into the church foyer, I heard my then four-year-old shrieking. My husband turned the corner, holding my son with half a box of tissues pressed to his head and soaked through with crimson-colored blood.

Tossing a football, my oldest son, Walker, had fallen and hit his head on a table. Life just happens, and sometimes you end up with stitches that ruin your future modeling career.

When my youngest son, Hudson, was fifteen months old, he fell down in the driveway and nearly broke his front tooth in half. He wasn't doing anything crazy, just toddling along as fifteen-month-old kids do. As gravity pulled his body forward, his legs struggled to stay underneath him, but they just couldn't.

I didn't know that teeth can actually bleed. For the record, they can ... especially if they break mostly in half.

While there are plenty of people in the world without teeth, I think it's fair to say that when a tooth that's front and center is gone, it doesn't exactly escape notice.

Several months and several hundred dollars later, after having a crown put on a fifteen-month-old, which, for the record, was *awful*,

Hudson somehow managed to knock the dang tooth enough times that we were forced to have it pulled.

A couple of years ago, on my way out the door to help host a movie screening, Hudson tripped again down two stairs in our den and smashed his face into the corner of the wall. His forehead split wide open and started gushing blood everywhere. After loading both kids in the car and calling my husband in a panic, I raced to the hospital, where my son ended up with several stitches.

When we moved into our most recent house, the previous owners left the trampoline because it wouldn't disassemble. I honestly felt fear in the pit in my stomach. DANGER! *Alert! Alert!*

Our dentist told me that, in some ways, trampolines keep him in business from all the knees knocking teeth deep into nasal cavities. Or, as our orthopedic friend says, they do *tons* of surgeries on the knees and joints of people who get hurt at the local trampoline park.

"So, do you want the trampoline?" the real estate agent asked me.

"Ummm … I really don't want it," I admitted. "Because of, you know, the DANGER!" *Bum-bum buuuummmm!*

I hung up the phone and remembered teeth being knocked out in the driveway. Then I remembered my son tripping down the stairs and busting his head open. Then I recalled him tossing a football and getting even more stitches. The DANGER … it's *everywhere!*

I dialed the Realtor back on second thought and said, "I think it can stay."

The first day I went outside with my kids, we jumped and laughed and played for well over an hour on the trampoline. I decided that the danger, while present, was causing me to overworry about unknown outcomes more than anything else. Playing that day yielded a whole lot more good than it would have if my worry had defined it all.

Maybe a trampoline is a bad example, because it does carry some real risk. But so does driving a car or flying in a plane. So does riding a horse. (I fell off one a couple of times in the past.) Or swimming in the ocean. (Hello, shark attack!) And so does sleeping. (I rolled off the top bunk in college.)

Y'all, for real, I've torn the entire butt off a pair of pants roller-blading. I've bruised the fire out of myself trying to learn how to snowboard. I've had water go up my nose while waterskiing till I choked and sputtered. The one time in my life when I gambled just to try it, I lost money on a horse race and then won it back on another. Jeremy and I have bought new cars with issues and old cars without. I've had my heart broken into a zillion little pieces because I loved someone who didn't know what it meant to love me back. I've had friendships break and seen life stolen from people too young. Right now I'm a little worried about an oddly shaped mole that recently appeared on my nose. So much of life just feels like a gamble.

All that worry, though, mostly comes down to me just being afraid. Afraid to hurt. Afraid to feel broken. Afraid to lose. Afraid to fail. Afraid of rejection. Afraid to die. I worry about what if: What if I do get hurt? Feel broken? Lose? Fail? Get rejected? Die? Do I believe that God can redeem those things or not? Do I believe that He will paint with beautiful intentionality on my life just as He does on the flowers?

The weird thing about worry is that it creates a scenario in our minds that isn't of the Lord. We focus on a lie from the enemy that stops our forward progress and makes us project something into the future that isn't a reality. We consider possibility—not the possibility of hope but possibilities rooted in death and loss. We root ourselves in a place that is void of truth and project negativity into a nebulous future. From there we avoid potential pain, and in doing so, we lose the capacity to be curious about things that could bring life.

Worry stunts faith because it convinces us not to trust God. But when we trust in the power of the One who puts everything together in the first place, we can trust that the things that break us won't define us.

What are you worried about? What keeps you up at night? Do you believe that God is big enough to address your worries? Your fears? Do you believe that He can overcome them? Do you believe that with Him you can? What nebulous future do you imagine? How does your story play out to the end when you allow your worries to take over?

FISHERS AND HUNTERS

Nothing in my life has the capacity to repeatedly incite fear like pregnancy. Nothing has quite compared with the dread of what could happen and the ache of loss that comes with carrying an unborn child. My medical history would tell you that it should have terrified me every single time.

I've been pregnant six times. Six. I have two kids to show for all those months of aching, wearing maternity clothes, and puking my guts out. Two kids is one heck of a blessing, but that doesn't mean I don't still grieve the loss of those other babies. Somehow, by what I can attribute only to the kindness of the Lord, I wasn't ever worried about losing a single one of those pregnancies. Maybe you're thinking I'm either a liar or stupid, but let me set the record straight: I'm neither.

Seriously, though, for all six pregnancies, I never really thought I'd lose any of them. Didn't even consider it. Even after we lost that first baby, when I got pregnant again, I was completely surprised when I started bleeding and miscarried just a few weeks in. It's not that I was in denial; I just never really thought it would happen again and again. Pregnant with my youngest, I never worried that he wouldn't be okay. By the fifth pregnancy, I was still pretty caught off guard when I miscarried just twenty-four hours after taking a test and getting used to the idea that I was pregnant again. And for that sixth baby, well, even up to the twelve-week mark, I didn't worry. And after the end of the first trimester, everyone said I didn't much need to worry anymore anyhow.

I guess maybe I just believed that I really couldn't add an hour to my life, or my baby's, by worrying. It was gonna be how it was gonna be, so I did my part to be healthy and knew I couldn't live well if I was worried all the time.

But I hadn't worried prior to this anyhow, so I just carried on, fattening up and puking and eating Kraft Macaroni & Cheese, since my friend Jenny Reeves told me it was the only thing that didn't hurt to throw up. (She was right, by the way.) And every time I ran out of church or jumped out of the car to hurl in my driveway, I guess I just counted my blessings between moans, because supposedly lots of puking means you're having a healthy pregnancy. I was puking like a champ, so I wasn't worrying. I just toted my ginger ale and ate saltine crackers at midnight, because despite my reservations about the actual truth behind those remedies, they did in fact help. I lived all happy, slappy, and pregnant.

I couldn't wait to find out the baby's gender. My husband and I learned the genders of both our boys by sixteen weeks, so Dr. Keller said we could peek at the ultrasound for this baby too.

I'll spare you the tears this go-round, but if you need to know how that appointment went, feel free to imagine yourself four weeks further along, securely into your second trimester, and then go back and reread the first part of chapter 1.

There was no blinking on the ultrasound screen this time either.

And I hadn't worried one minute. Jeremy and I prayed and prayed over that baby. We felt like the Lord told us to name this child Fisher because he or she would be a fisher of men for the kingdom of heaven. We heard promises and held tightly on to hope and truth and life, and I hadn't worried one single bit that it wouldn't all come to pass. And praise the Lord for that, because the aftermath of yet another loss was enough to stomach: two D & Cs (because I had complications this time) and a month's worth of Methergine, pain meds, and nausea, not to mention still having to wear maternity clothes, since my regular ones didn't fit. The disappointment and pain this time were worse than ever. I yelled and cursed at God. I kicked and screamed and blamed Him. I called Him a liar for giving me a name like Fisher for a baby who would never live to see the light of day, much less ever lead people to the Lord. How could I have been so stupid not to worry? But even if I had, it wouldn't have changed a single thing. I'd still have been fat and sad and empty wombed.

Did I tell you that the first baby we lost we named Hunter? Hunter and Fisher—the first and last of my babies who died. The only two of four who made it to the second trimester. Until Fisher died, I never really realized we'd done that, given them names that had to do with gathering.

A week after Fisher died, I forced myself to walk to the front of the sanctuary during a Sunday service to sit on the floor and worship. I forced myself to get up because, *especially because*, nothing in me wanted to do anything even close to that. What reason did I have to praise God? I had lots of dead babies. And as I sat and wept, I opened my Bible somehow to Jeremiah. I think it was one of those times when I just ran my finger down a page and stopped somewhere random.

I found myself pointing to a section titled "The LORD Will Restore Israel." Anyhow, as I read, I noticed this:

> Behold, I am sending for many fishers, declares the
> LORD, and they shall catch [the people of Israel].
> And afterward I will send for many hunters, and they
> shall hunt them from every mountain and every hill,
> and out of the clefts of the rocks. (16:16)

Fishers and hunters … in the same verse … talking about rescue. *But how, Lord, can dead babies be fishers and hunters? How, Lord, can what nearly destroyed me bring about my rescue?*

I pulled up a Bible commentary on my phone right there on the floor of the sanctuary to learn more about the fishers and hunters. It said,

The Chaldees were famous in hunting, as the Egyptians ... were in fishing. "Fishers" expresses the ease of their victory over the Jews as that of the angler over fishes; "hunters," the keenness of their pursuit of them into every cave and nook. It is remarkable, the same image is used in a good sense of the Jews' restoration, implying that just as their enemies were employed by God to take them in hand for destruction, so the same shall be employed for their restoration [Ezra 47:9–10]. So spiritually, those once enemies by nature ... were employed by God to be heralds of salvation, "catching men" for life.[1]

As with Israel, the same things the enemy had planned for my destruction, the Lord would employ for my restoration. Instead of pushing me into a lifetime of worry, my Fisher and Hunter could continue to bring hope and restoration, whether I got to hold them or not.

I won't patronize you by saying that it all turned out just fine, because the truth is that there are days when it's still hard to accept that my family isn't what I thought it would be. But just as I can't allow worry about the danger to define the way I make decisions to live a full life with my living children, I can't allow fears of loss to rule my life either. I don't know what will happen in this life, but if I live all my days in fear and worry of what might be, I'll miss out on so much of the goodness that I can have today.

Spending our days in worry wastes the potential blessings God has for us. Fear that paralyzes us from moving forward also stops us short of God's goodness and deliverance. When worry yells loud, silence it with rejoicing over the blessings in your life. God says not to be anxious but to bring our worries and our burdens to Him. He will trade the heavy things in our lives for a measure of His peace. Paul hit another good thought out of the park in Philippians 4:4–7 when he said:

> Rejoice in the Lord always; again I will say, rejoice. Let your reasonableness be known to everyone. The Lord is at hand; do not be anxious about anything, but in everything by prayer and supplication with thanksgiving let your requests be made known to God. And the peace of God, which surpasses all understanding, will guard your hearts and your minds in Christ Jesus.

As believers in Christ, we have no business being pessimists. We can't be defined by our worries over what could go wrong. Make no mistake, things *will* go wrong, but we can't live in perpetual fear just waiting for brokenness. We live in a fallen world, so broken is going to happen. We can't allow the fear of it to chart our paths forward, though.

If an optimist is defined as "someone who looks at the world like a glass half-full," then when even our rock bottom is positive, we'll never be found half-empty.

Martin Seligman, a social psychologist and author of the book *Learned Optimism*, says that optimists are people who come back stronger after defeat.

If you believe that Jesus Christ died, was buried, and was resurrected to bring you new life, then, my friend, you subscribe to a theology that hinges on coming back stronger after defeat. Which means that worry is nothing more than a lie that gets in your way, slows you down, and prevents you from living out the redemption, possibility, and blessings God has for you.

Root yourself deep in the truth that God promises to never leave you or forsake you (see Josh. 1:5). Remember, God is good, and He is for you. Claim the optimism and hope that were given to you in Christ's resurrection and redemption. Don't waste your life in fear and worry when you have a God who is in the business of renewal, rescue, hope, and possibility. Don't worry about the future; be curious about it! Because God loves you and has some goodness for you!

Chapter 7
Waiting Well

You'll escape all that waiting and staying … find the
bright places where Boom Bands are playing.

Dr. Seuss, *Oh, the Places You'll Go!*

"I'm sorry, ma'am. Your passport isn't valid."

"Yes, it is. It doesn't expire until July. It's March."

"Well, to enter Uganda, your passport has to be valid at least six months past the travel dates. It's different for different countries, but your travel agent should have told you that."

"She didn't."

"Well, then, I'm sorry. We cannot issue your ticket." The response was so matter-of-fact. Negotiation was clearly not an option.

Tears filled my eyes and dripped down my hot cheeks as I stood, motionless. The heartache of disappointment threading through my insides, jumbling emotion with little-known facts and piles of misunderstanding and misinformation. It all felt messy and confusing.

A knot the size of my clenched fists trapped the air desperate to escape my lungs. My pride and sensibility somehow held back the loud wails of lost hope that threatened to dramatize my already shocking circumstance.

I'd been planning for months to make the inaugural trip to Africa with my dear friends at Sole Hope, which is a ministry and aid organization serving the poor and underprivileged children of Uganda. I joined a team to see firsthand the work that Sole Hope is doing to provide medical treatment and shoes to children. Our primary objective was to write the stories and be a voice for the people there who don't have the ability to tell the world themselves.

Not renewing my passport was a conscious decision. After all, it didn't expire until July, and we were going to Uganda in March. It would be easier just to send it in when I returned home and get it back in time for a late-summer trip. There would be plenty of time then, so I wouldn't have to pay the fees to expedite it. But no matter how conscious my decision making had been, nothing could have prepared me for the wave of emotion that surfaced.

"I'm sorry. We cannot issue your ticket." Whether the words were intended to cement the meaning in my mind or simply move me away from the ticket counter, they accomplished both.

"It's going to be okay. We'll make a couple of phone calls and get this all sorted out. It'll just take a few minutes. I'm sure this is a misunderstanding." My friend Wynne's words were kind, even if they held little real hope.

The rest of the team rushed to reassure me. We would all still be removing our shoes and hefting our carry-on bags onto the conveyer belt at the security check-in any minute, right?

But I knew. I wasn't going with them to Africa.

My hopes and dreams sat pooled at my feet, mingling with the salty water that wouldn't stop trailing down my cheeks.

WAITING IN EXILE

When I was growing up, my mom recited this Scripture passage to me all the time:

> For I know the plans I have for you, declares the LORD, plans for welfare and not for evil, to give you a future and a hope. Then you will call upon me and come and pray to me, and I will hear you. You will seek me and find me, when you seek me with all your heart. (Jer. 29:11–13)

Mom shared it unsolicited with my sister and brother too. She meant well by it, to be sure, but it grated on my nerves. Then I became a grown-up, and I swear that everyone else I met started saying it all the time too. If things weren't going the way I thought they should, or if I looked like I needed some encouragement … it hardly needed an intro; it seemed that everyone could find a reason to apply Jeremiah 29:11–13 to pretty much every situation in the history of ever.

When you're a newly minted adult, fresh out of college, it really becomes the mission of everyone older and wiser to give sage advice. Reciting that passage was a churchy way of saying, "You don't have to know what's going on in your life. But God does, and it's all going to work out just peachy. Cheers! Blessings! Traveling mercies!"

Whatever. Perhaps I shouldn't confess it, but this scripture annoyed the fire out of me for years.

Tell me I'm not alone! You've probably had this scripture dumped on you like a surprise tank of icy water too, right? When you're worried or stressed or confused … or waiting to make sense of things. People dump it on you especially when you're waiting.

One day I just got so darn sick of hearing it that I decided to read a little more to try to figure out what in the world was going on when Jeremiah wrote these words. Surely there was something about this scripture that wasn't soaked in saccharine-rich encouragement. Perhaps a little history lesson would help unpack things for me.

I learned that beginning around 597 BC, Babylon's king Nebuchadnezzar laid siege to Jerusalem and eventually captured it. Assuming power and extending Babylonian rule in the land, he destroyed Solomon's temple and took most of the prominent Israelites back to Babylon as captives. Over time he captured and exiled more people from their homelands. His triumph over the kingdom of Judah pretty much destroyed the Hebrew nation and scattered the Jewish people all over. For more than seventy years, the Israelites were exiled from their homelands and held in captivity in Babylon. Basically the entire nation of Israel was in a hot mess of confusion. Exiled and waiting to figure out what would happen to them next.

When the prophet Jeremiah penned his letter to the Israelites, he wrote it as they were in this place of waiting—waiting to figure out their fate, waiting to find a home, waiting on their hopes for a future.

Speaking through Jeremiah, God basically said to the people, "I know the plans I have for you, and they aren't to keep you in this mess. No, they're for good. They're full of future and hope. You aren't going to be trapped in exile forever, because you're not just waiting to leave this place; you're waiting on *Me*, God. When you wait on Me, you'll find Me for sure."

Suddenly the passage didn't bother me so much anymore. When God promises a future and a hope, He is also talking about delivery from exile. This isn't just a sappy "I have happy plans for you" sort of verse. It's a promise of deliverance. It's God promising us that when we come to Him to pray, to search Him out, even in the midst of exile, we will find Him. If He can promise that in exile, I know He promises the same while we're just waiting.

Do we believe that even in the midst of waiting for promises or dreams to come to pass, God wants what is good for us? But how do we wait well? When hope is deferred and our best-laid plans don't seem even sort of within reach, how do we hang on? How do we keep from losing heart? From falling prey to continued disappointment and discouragement? What does it look like to wait well?

In the same ways that fear projects potential loss into a nebulous future, waiting can rob us of hope. When we're forced to wait for outcomes, if fear doesn't grip us, then doubting God's goodness often does. When we doubt His desire to bless us, to give us a hope and a future, waiting can leave us feeling awfully hopeless.

Remember when we talked about the wilderness in chapter 5? Well, waiting can sure feel like its own version of wilderness, can't it? But just as we don't want to waste our wilderness, we don't want to waste our waiting either. It's a space between where I am and where I want to be. The wait is what separates us from achieved dreams, met longings, and hope fulfilled. It's all the life that happens until we get what we've been wanting. It can be an impatient-feeling place.

Yet we have to remember, especially in that place, that God makes a way in the wilderness and rivers in the desert. It's a curious faith that helps us find the way. If we can focus our expectations not on what we hope will happen but on the idea of meeting the Lord in the midst of our longing, we'll discover that waiting can actually be a place full of joy.

KILLING TIME IS KILLING ME

I gathered my thoughts through pouring tears at the Delta ticket counter, opened my spirit wide, and wrapped it around the idea that I might not actually be going to Africa that March day. Realizing that this could be the moment I would climb into my car and drive three hours northward back home left my heart full of heavy disappointment.

It felt as if heavy bricks of lost hope sat crushing on my chest.

Either you trust Me or you don't. Which is it?

It wasn't an audible voice from God, but it might as well have been. My mind pulsed around the faith I had clung to so tightly for most of my life. Tears slowed, and something new tensed within me when I realized that the words actually required an answer.

But how can I go? It takes weeks to get a passport. Even if I could, I've never been to Africa, let alone by myself!

I wasn't that brave.

I'm the girl who sleeps with an eye half-open when my husband is out of town. The same girl who makes audible "ouch" sounds watching my son take hits to the chest pad in a lacrosse match for eight-year-olds. I'm the woman who holds my car key "just so" between my knuckles, walking through the grocery-store parking lot late at night. You know, just in case.

I've always been kind of a wuss.

Africa ... alone? Not me, Lord. Surely You mean someone else.

After all, even Moses punted to Aaron, right? "Oh, my Lord, please send someone else" (Exod. 4:13).

"Yes, you, Moses. You're the one I want for this mission," God told him.

But I'm not Moses. I'm just me, the girl who thinks sheets pulled high over my head really can hide me from late-night creaks in contracting wooden floors. Thank heavens this scenario was only about one person getting on an airplane to Africa, not leading legions of people out of slavery.

I trust You, Lord, my heart sighed. Not leaning into understanding but clinging to faith in the knowledge that God doesn't always call the equipped, but He does equip the called. If I knew nothing else at that moment, I knew that He was good and that He was for me. A curiosity ignited deep in my heart as I waited to see what His plans would be.

This particular equipping, however, would require nothing short of a complete move of God.

As I stood in the airport, trying to process the magnitude of not boarding a plane that day, I called my dear old friend Alexis for help. She *just happened* to do contract work for Delta. She also *just happened* to be in the international terminal of the Atlanta Hartsfield airport at that moment. At ... that ... moment.

Four minutes later, my childhood friend stood next to me. *Four minutes!*

Before I knew what was happening, Alexis was confidently speaking on the phone with someone from the airline. Sole Hope's executive assistant, Holly, was also there making calls. The team circled around me, laid hands on my trembling shoulders, and began to pray.

Minutes later I was standing in a line to talk to another ticket agent. Though it didn't make sense, a new resolve embraced my fragile heart. I looked across the room, blew a kiss, and waved a silent good-bye to the seven women I should have been walking beside as they moved out of view toward a plane bound for Africa.

No matter how I sliced it, no matter how ideal the situation could play out from then on, the reality staring me in the face was that I was going to be waiting. There was also a very real chance that I wouldn't be going at all.

Somewhere amid the fresh resolve that took residence in my heart, I remembered Shadrach, Meshach, and Abednego in the Bible. These three men knew what they were called to do, in opposition to King Nebuchadnezzar, who ordered them to worship a golden image. These men also knew the character of God and trusted Him more than their own fears about the threat of impending punishment or death. They told the king,

> If this be so, our God whom we serve is able to
> deliver us from the burning fiery furnace, and he
> will deliver us out of your hand, O king. But if not,
> be it known to you, O king, that we will not serve
> your gods or worship the golden image that you
> have set up. (Dan. 3:17–18)

Even if I wouldn't be going to Uganda, I knew that God was still good and that He was still for me. I wasn't being asked to deny my convictions or walk into a fiery furnace; I was being asked only to wait. So even though I was faced with disappointment, I was gripped with the knowledge that God was still good. My going to Uganda wasn't the determiner of God's goodness.

Our disappointment doesn't nullify the inherent goodness of God. Even death doesn't defy His goodness and mercy. The kindness of God towers above the threats and pains of this earth and drips down the bruised flesh of a man named Jesus hanging from a tree. My disappointment paled in the light of His ultimate goodness.

While my heart cried out to walk in the paths of the promises I believed were set before me, I realized that perhaps the waiting itself could reveal something greater for me. Maybe killing time wasn't the worst thing that could happen.

After leaving the airport with no ticket, I spent the night at the house of my friend Alexis. I felt restless in her little blue house, switching from sofa to floor and back to sofa again, which kept my mind going crazy despite my best attempts to sleep. Every hour passed before my eyes—12:15, 1:15, 2:15. My body's internal clock ticked off the minutes with the accuracy of a stopwatch. Hours rolled by, and the white light on my phone showed 4:15 a.m. I finally rolled over, plugged headphones in my ears, and closed my eyes to listen to some worship music.

Because sometimes life just feels like a big waiting room. It makes a soul restless. It's frustrating. Waiting is hard. Waiting can be so boring. Will we ever see what we spend so much time waiting for?

We wait in lines to check out at the store. We wait in rooms with cold cloths pressed onto foreheads of sick children needing to be seen by a doctor. We wait for job offers and for "the one" to come along and sweep us off our feet with a marriage proposal. We wait for babies to be born and death to eventually rob people we love of life.

Life on this earth won't ever be lived without waiting. So we'd better figure out how to wait well.

THE JOY OF WAITING

For most of my life, I thought waiting was about killing time. A passive way to spend the interim between here and there. Twiddling thumbs in the line at the post office. Rocking in a chair on the porch at Cracker Barrel till a waitress calls your name for a table. Those things frustrate me, though. It's just delaying my preferred outcome.

I read a book called *The McDonaldization of Society* for a sociology class in college. It was about how our culture has basically trained us to expect efficiency to such an extent that it robs us of experience. The emergence of fast-food restaurants has taught us to replace tradition, values, and emotions. We sacrifice interaction for calculated outcomes for behavior. In the midst of all this, we've trained ourselves to function impatiently. Over time we've taught ourselves that waiting is bad.

But as it turns out, waiting *with* God is something else entirely.

The darkness of the night and hope unfulfilled surrounded me on the gray carpet in Alexis's living room. Somehow, as songs of praise rang through my ears, hope began to rise in my spirit.

I reached for my phone in the darkness, opened a Bible app, and keyed in the words "wait on the Lord." The search pulled up a list of verses. I began opening each of them, moving methodically down the list, verse after verse after verse.

> I believe that I shall look upon the goodness
> of the LORD
> in the land of the living!
> *Wait* for the LORD;
> be strong, and let your heart take courage;
> *wait* for the LORD! (Ps. 27:13–14)

> Be strong, and let your heart take courage,
> all you who *wait* for the LORD! (Ps. 31:24)

> *Wait* for the LORD and keep his way,
> and he will exalt you to inherit the land.
> (Ps. 37:34)

> But for you, O LORD, do I *wait*;
> it is you, O LORD my God, who will
> answer. (Ps. 38:15)

> He gives power to the faint,
> and to him who has no might he increases
> strength.
> Even youths shall faint and be weary,
> and young men shall fall exhausted;

> but they who *wait* for the LORD shall renew
>> their strength;
> they shall mount up with wings like
>> eagles;
> they shall run and not be weary;
>> they shall walk and not faint.
>> (Isa. 40:29–31)

For in this hope we were saved. Now hope that is seen is not hope. For who hopes for what he sees? But if we hope for what we do not see, we *wait* for it with patience. (Rom. 8:24–25)

Be strong. Be courageous. Inherit the land. Run and don't be weary. Be strong and take courage. Wait for the Lord and see His goodness in the land of the living.

Waiting is courageous. Waiting is brave. Waiting is active. Waiting is full of experience along the way. It's not a void we're stuck in until something new happens. It doesn't make us victims of circumstances we can't change. Waiting is growing and pursuit. Waiting cultivates strength and rich experience.

Nehemiah was right on when he said that the joy of the Lord is our strength (Neh. 8:10). And then over and over the psalmists echoed the same thing. If waiting is strong, then waiting can and should produce joy. Waiting can be hard, but it can also be joyful.

My friend Ann Voskamp cultivates joy and thankfulness in counting blessings. In her book *One Thousand Gifts: A Dare to Live Fully Right Where You Are*, Ann embraces everyday blessings and embarks on the transformative spiritual discipline of chronicling God's gifts. If we can experience the goodness of God in all the thousands of gifts surrounding us, then we begin to live more fully and cultivate a heart of thankfulness. Start counting: sunlight on your windowsill ... the sounds of laughter when your children get the giggles at bedtime ... apple pie ... soft sheets ... the stranger in the grocery-store parking lot who returned your cart in the rain. Start counting the gifts and watch your thankfulness multiply.

Multiply your thankfulness, and you'll multiply your joy. And according to the Scriptures, joy produces strength, which is good because waiting requires strength.

God showed me there in the middle of that dark room (not on a plane to Uganda), amid twisted blankets piled around me on the floor, that my waiting can be full of joy when my heart is filled with thanks.

Thankfulness multiplies when I chronicle the goodness of the Father in my life. When I notice it. When I write it down. When I look for all the blessings around me.

Lying there on the shag carpet at Alexis's house, I began thanking God for everything I could think of. I thanked Him that Alexis was at the airport that day ... for the friendly fella who didn't make me feel ugly, despite the fact I'd been crying before I took a new passport picture at CVS ... for the eggplant Parmesan Alexis had the ingredients to make ... that Holly could stay with me at Alexis's house that night ... that my local friend Amena was willing to take me to the passport office the next day ... for a soft place to sleep and friends who prayed.

Hope began to rise around me when I focused on God's goodness. When I thought of the gifts of my family, husband, and children, of home and friends, and of opportunities to even think of going to Africa in the first place, I felt my entire countenance begin to change.

Even though I was disappointed that I wasn't taking the trip I'd been planning, getting into the car to go back home wasn't the worst thing in the world anymore either. Heaps and heaps of blessings waited for me there too. Blessing was heaped around me even there on the floor.

Somewhere in the middle of counting blessings like counting sheep jumping over a fence, I finally closed my eyes and fell asleep, not to be woken until an alarm on my phone sounded a couple of hours later.

The next morning, Alexis, Holly, and I all hopped into the car to go to the US passport office in Atlanta. I counted the blessing that there even was a passport office in Atlanta!

We grabbed a coffee and headed upstairs, where I plopped on the floor outside the office to wait and hope I could get in to renew my passport without an appointment. A twentysomething fella heading to Cancun for spring break was in front of me in line. Like me, he'd failed to renew his passport in time. He hadn't even looked at the expiration date until he went to leave.

Spring break in Cancun … ugh. I was trying to go to Africa to help people. I felt ugliness rise up in my chest and immediately squashed it. I prayed for favor for him to go on his trip. I thanked God for the coffee shop just below the passport office. I thanked Him again for Holly and Alexis and my friend Amena, who were helping me through the crazy process.

I stared at a line of about twenty-five people opposite me in the hallway. All of them had appointments. I counted my chances and felt disappointment. I counted my blessings and felt hopeful.

"Come on, y'all," I heard a woman in a security uniform call into the hallway.

Spring Breaker and I stayed seated cross-legged on the floor.

"You too," the woman said and motioned toward our side of the hallway.

Spring Breaker and I exchanged looks of disbelief. "This must be good," he said to me as we both shrugged and moved toward the security station.

I sent my things through the X-ray machine and gave my name to the next guard as he jotted it down and handed me a number. Then I entered the passport office and chose a seat somewhere in the middle of the room.

It felt like the DMV. I've always waited an eternity at the DMV, and that's just for a driver's license.

Minutes later—*minutes!*—a woman called my number and waved me to her window. She took my passport and some information and told me I owed $179.

"Wait! You're charging me?" I nearly shouted.

"Yes, ma'am. It'll be one hundred seventy-nine dollars, please." She looked at me as if to say, "Of course I'm charging you!"

"But if you're charging me, then does that mean I get my passport today? That means I get it, right?"

"Yes. You just come back at about two o'clock, and it'll be ready for pickup."

"Today? You mean at two o'clock today? I'll have my new passport *today*?"

I was practically jumping up and down.

"If I could hug you through this window right now, I would," I told her. "You've made my day! I'm so thankful for you, and I hope you experience more blessings today than any day this week! You just made my day!"

Her face softened as she smiled and said, "Honey, you're going to have a new passport *today*!"

I'm thankful that people in the South call you "honey." It makes good news taste even sweeter. I counted that blessing too.

Amena picked me up for lunch, and we returned a couple of hours later to get my new passport. Before I knew it, I was headed back to the airport to see if I could fly standby on the same flight I'd missed just twenty-four hours earlier.

If the Atlanta airport had been the Red Sea, I'm convinced that it would have parted that day.

Amena and I walked into the international terminal, and the first person I saw was Natasha, the Delta agent I'd joked with the day before as we began checking in. She had given me a hug when we realized I wasn't going to be joining my team on our original flight.

"Natasha!" I shouted and walked up to her.

"Logan!" She remembered my name, and I thanked God for that too.

"Baby girl, let's get you on a plane to Africa!" she exclaimed.

"Well, Natasha, we rebooked the flight for Wednesday because we didn't know how long it might take for me to get a new passport. And I wanted to have some extra time. But I got it today! So what are the chances I can get on the flight tonight? When we called Delta earlier, they said if I change it back to tonight, it would cost six thousand dollars. What are the chances I can fly standby?"

"Lemme see what I can do, honey."

There it was again. *Honey*—sweet words from Natasha, who remembered my name. I uttered more thanks in my spirit. I kept feeling stronger, more courageous, and more hopeful despite the fact that nothing was certain.

Put one foot in front of the other, Logan. You don't know where this is going, but just keep thanking. Keep walking. Be strong and courageous and wait on the Lord. My mind kept repeating what my heart needed to hear.

Forty-five minutes later, I boarded a full plane to Amsterdam. I snagged the last seat on a flight that should have cost me six thousand dollars. In Amsterdam, a friendly flight attendant named Heidi welcomed me onto the plane for Entebbe, Uganda. She could see I was exhausted and whispered into my ear that the plane was hardly full. As soon as they turned off the Fasten Seat Belts sign, I could move up and stretch out to sleep across a middle row of five seats!

As I stretched out across the row, I thanked God for $179 in passport fees; for Alexis, Holly, and Amena; for Natasha greeting me; for the last seat on a "full" flight; and for a place to sleep well before arriving alone in a foreign land. While it didn't make sense, I realized that in the insanity of a twenty-four-hour span of time, I never felt worried. I knew in the end, no matter what happened, it would be okay. A light at the end of a tunnel isn't the ultimate destination. We've been given a torch of faith to walk through a tunnel when we can't see where we're going, and thankfulness along the way makes us brave.

"We walk by faith, not by sight" (2 Cor. 5:7). One foot in front of the other. One thankful word before another. Where waiting isn't purgatory but is strong and courageous and joyful.

DON'T SELL YOUR ONIONS TOO FAST

In one of my favorite books ever, *Radical Hospitality,* Lonni Pratt tells a story that continues to make an impression on me. While it wasn't about waiting in her context, I can't help but consider that the overall premise of her book totally applies to the goodness I believe that God has for us as we wait in our own lives.

> Go with [me] to a corner of the sprawling market in Mexico City where an old Indian man named Pota-lamo is selling onions. Twenty strings of onions lay in front of him. A guy from Denver walks up and asks, "How much for a string of onions?"
>
> "Ten cents," replies Pota-lamo.
>
> "How much for two strings?"
>
> Pota-lamo fixes his eyes on him and says, "Twenty cents."
>
> "What about three?"
>
> "Thirty cents."
>
> "Not much of a reduction for quantity. Would you take twenty-five cents for three?"
>
> "No."
>
> "Well, how much for all of it, the whole twenty strings?"
>
> "I will not sell you the whole twenty strings."
>
> "Why not?" asks the American. "Aren't you here to sell onions?"

"No," replies Pota-lamo, "I am here to live my
life. I love this market. I love the crowds. I love the
sunlight and smells. I love the children. I love to
have my friends come by and talk about their babies
and their crops. That is my life and for that reason I
sit with my twenty strings of onions. If I sell all my
onions to one customer, then my day is over and I
have lost my life that I love—and that I will not do."[1]

Of course, when we have goals, time passes until we achieve
them. But I want to be like Pota-lamo. I don't want to miss all the
goodness that happens while I'm waiting to sell the onions of my life.
I want to look beyond the things I hope for to see the fullness that
fills up all the space between.

What are you waiting for? Can you believe with me that our good
God has more for us than accomplishing only what we want or hope
for? Life in the marketplace is overflowing if we focus on the blessing
along the way rather than becoming distracted by outcomes.

Listen, I know that waiting twenty-four hours to go to Africa is
a cakewalk compared to waiting years to become pregnant, or to get
married, or to come out on the other side of cancer. I've spent time
waiting on those things too. And it is *hard*. But I know that the lessons
the Lord showed me on Alexis's floor still apply when hours turn to
days and days turn to months and months turn to years. Time can
feel so slow when we're waiting for answers and outcomes. When all I
can imagine is a certain end, will I trust that what God has for me in
between is good? Will I believe that He really does desire to give me a
hope and a future?

Can we look beyond our plans enough to find thankfulness and gratitude in the waiting? Our thankfulness will produce a new joy, which converts to strength that we're going to need if we're to be courageous and wait. To wait on the Lord is to renew it all. Soak in His goodness and know that the hope you carry is rooted in the truth of heaven, not the fruition of earthly hopes. Are you willing to be curious enough while you wait to wonder what God may be up to? Curious enough to wonder what He may be preparing you for?

Waiting isn't a delay of the thing we have in our mind's eye. It's about being present in the now and placing a longing hope in God. It's the space in which we root ourselves in truth and learn to want God more than our own desires.

By the way, in 539 BC, Babylon fell to Persia. The king of Persia, Cyrus II, not only permitted more than fifty thousand Jews to return home to Israel and rebuild the temple, but also restored all the treasure Nebuchadnezzar had taken from them. Of course, the full history of Israel is significantly more complicated. Still, the exiles' fortunes were restored, and they returned home. Hope and a future were theirs indeed. Perhaps for us to enjoy the greatest restoration and fulfillment, God wants us to discover hope in Him through the waiting.

Chapter 8

Settling for Good

*There is no passion to be found playing small—in settling for
a life that is less than the one you are capable of living.*

Nelson Mandela

When I moved away from home to go to school, I remember
picking out bedding and setting up my dorm room to reflect
bits and pieces of my personality. The dorm bed came fitted
with a standard blue-and-white-striped mattress. It was more a
Princess-and-the-Pea sort of thinly veiled comfort than it was a
Goldilocks-and-the-baby-bear level of perfect softness. So my
parents bought a foam egg crate to help take the edge off the dis-
comfort of a cheap mattress.

My friend Cydney put a feather mattress on her bed, which was
the softest and fluffiest bed in all of Perkins dormitory. She came
to school prepared, and we all figured out pretty quickly that she
had the right idea. So I asked for a feather mattress for my birthday
the following year. Some other holiday or birthday down the line, I

asked for soft sheets and pillows. Over time my bed became my own little retreat of cozy softness.

All through college and during my single years afterward, I perfected the cloud-like comfort of my bed. A fresh, fluffy mattress and pillows topped by soft sheets became a haven that brought me pride and comfort.

Shortly after I turned twenty-five and got married, my husband began to grumble about the squishy goodness that was my sleepy oasis of joy.

"This bed makes me so hot!" he said. "There are too many covers and pillows! The feather mattress hurts my back! Can we please get rid of all this extra stuff?"

In the early days of our marriage, I relented and gave up my castle on a cloud for the sake of compromise with the man I loved. But for nearly the next twelve years, I looked back on the days of my perfect bed and wished for its return. Let's be honest. I nagged my husband for its return.

"I miss my squishy bed. Oh, to return to the days of pillowy softness. If only I could have my cloud-castle bed back. This bed is so hard." Grumble, grumble, complain, complain.

Despite the removal of all my cushy happiness, my husband continued to experience neck and back pain, mostly resulting from old college football injuries.

Recently I announced to him, from the depths of my own understanding and compassion, most assuredly, that if his back was going to hurt no matter what, then I wanted my fluffy bed back. After all, I'd compromised for well over a decade. Now it was my turn to have a blissful night's sleep. I know ... so much sympathy, right?

This time he agreed, and five minutes post-announcement, I received an online order confirmation that my four-inch feather mattress would arrive in two days. Because when you've been waiting for almost twelve years, you don't wait a single second longer than necessary to return things to their former glory.

When the mattress arrived, I immediately fluffed it and got it settled on the bed. I stretched freshly washed, soft sheets to cover the now-deeper mattress. Pillows were shaken and arranged. Sleepy perfection was within my grasp. I told my husband to stand back and admire it with me. I snapped a picture to commemorate the glorious occasion, took ten steps backward from the foot of the bed, and then ran and jumped right into the center. I slowly sunk deep into the fluff and slept like a baby that night.

Night two in my heavenly bed was similar in comfort, though, for whatever reason, I had a fitful night's sleep.

After night four I awoke with tension in my neck and lower back. But I conjectured that I was probably just stressed about something or other.

The morning after night five left me doing toe touches and sun salutations in the shower to stretch out the increasing tension in my back. My husband also complained that he was hot with all the fluff cradling him at night. I began to actually wonder if the mattress might be at the root of my new pains. So I graciously offered to keep the mattress on for only two months a year during the coldest season. That way, if it was the cause of my own back problems, I'd never have to admit it.

But when I woke up after night six and could hardly move, I realized that even my pride wouldn't be able to survive another eight weeks of misery that most definitely seemed to be linked to the cloud castle that was becoming my sleepy prison.

Standing in the closet thirty minutes after my husband left for work, I dialed his number and heard him pick up his end of the line.

"Hey, what's up?"

"Um … honey, I have a really serious confession. Something that brings me a huge amount of embarrassment but will likely bring you some level of deserved joy."

"Is everything okay? Are you all right, babe?"

"Well, no. See, the thing is that my back hurts … like *really, really* hurts. I can hardly move today. I think it's the feather mattress. I'm going to take it off. In fact, I know it's the problem. I haven't slept well in days, and my back hurts so stinking bad that I can't even walk today without pain. Oh my gosh, honey, it hurts so bad."

His compassion for my situation was quickly drowned out by hysterical laughter. "AHAHAHAHAHA! BWAAAHAAAA! Oh my gosh … that is amazing!"

But seriously, I couldn't blame him. I was facedown in a plate of humble pie and knew it. For years I lived in a memory of something that had formerly been glorious. But after nearly a dozen years, six pregnancies, a couple of C-sections interrupting my muscle configurations, irregular exercise routines, and a body that has stretched and changed with the seasons, my bones and muscles just don't seem to appreciate the things they used to love so much.

All those years I spent wishing that this part of my life would return to what it had been, living in the tension of what I'd had and still thought I wanted. Somewhere along the line, I became convinced that my life (and sleep) would be significantly better if I could just have it back the way it used to be. But I failed to realize that I had, in fact, been sleeping pretty comfortably for years.

Maybe for you it's round about year seven, fifteen, or thirty of your marriage, and you find your thoughts drifting back to "the one that got away" in college. You wonder if life would be better had you stayed together. Perhaps it's the dream job you gave up to stay close to family. Do you imagine being back in the place that felt so life giving to you for that season of your life? If only things could be as they were.

The truth is that no matter how we remember things, life happens in between. Often the stuff we spend years wanting back wouldn't fit us now that we've become the present version of ourselves. Marriage even with "the one that got away" would still be hard, because life is hard. That dream job would one day disappoint whether it was nearby or far from family and friends. Houses in other cities still have expensive plumbing repairs. Friends will let you down no matter what language they speak.

There is no ideal version of our imperfect lives, no matter how perfect they seem to be in our memories. Still, we can carry the tension as if an ideal version of life actually exists. When we settle for what we think is best, we lose our curiosity for anything God may have planned for us.

LICKABLE WALLPAPER

When I was a little girl, my bedroom was covered in wallpaper boasting pink-and-white stripes. Floral clusters strung together to fill the space between the vertical lines. And if the busy striped-and-floral combination wasn't elaborate enough, a pearlescent wood-grain moiré overlay enhanced the overall feel of elegance. It almost makes me laugh out loud now to think of that visually arresting disaster of pink pearlized pattern and texture covering the entire room. At the time, though, I thought it was magnificent.

I used to imagine that the wallpaper in my room was made of candy. I got the idea from watching my old favorite *Willy Wonka and the Chocolate Factory*, which has clearly been a source of inspiration for me. (See chapter 4 in case you forgot.) In the movie, there was a hallway of lickable wallpaper that reminded me of the intense striped pattern covering my own childhood room. Sometimes I taped long strips of colorful candy dots onto the walls and pretended that I lived in the hallway of lickable wallpaper. Because, really, what could be better? Lickable candy wallpaper was about the best thing I could imagine. Sweetness all around, flavors galore, all within reach. I could have just stopped right there and been happy forever.

Or so I thought.

Years later when I watched *Willy Wonka* again for that first inspiring time with my boys, I found myself thinking how much the lucky ticket holders would have missed had they stayed in that hallway of lickable goodness. I mean, it was good. There was no doubt about that. But if they had stayed there, they never would have walked into the room full of candy. They would have missed the whipped-cream mushrooms and the beach-ball-sized gumballs. They wouldn't have experienced the chocolate river or sipped tea from a daffodil cup. If the children hadn't trusted that the creator had more in store for them, they would have settled for good and never experienced the greatness of all that was to come.

Proverbs 16:9 says, "The heart of man plans his way, but the LORD establishes his steps."

It can be so hard, though, waiting on the things we desire. Maybe if we just scale back our hopes a bit? Perhaps our dreams are too lofty. We can't discern when our hopes are too high or our dreams are unrealistic, but the Lord can. When we listen to Him, when we curiously seek His heart for our lives, He will begin to uncover bits and pieces of what our future could hold. The apostle Paul advised:

> Look carefully then how you walk, not as unwise but as wise, making the best use of the time, because the days are evil. Therefore do not be foolish, but understand what the will of the Lord is. (Eph. 5:15–17)

At times I could spend days kicking myself for not pursuing the best option, but sometimes I just get lazy, I guess, and find myself thinking that "good" will be good enough. I'm willing to settle for less to reach my objective instead of pursuing the fullness and goodness God has for me.

Of course, we're all just trying to make the best decisions we can with the information before us, but deep inside, so often we know when we settle. We know when we're cutting corners, or tired of waiting, or just trying to find the simplest way to reach our destinations sooner than later.

How often do we jump at something before the time is right because we're so eager to achieve the result we have in mind?

How often do we miss out on the goodness we could experience, simply because we haven't learned how to wait well? How often do we settle for what seems good, when trusting God's heart for us could actually lead us to something great? It all comes back to the question of trust. Do we trust God enough to believe that what He has for us is good ... that what He has for us could even be *great*? Or do we think that just because an option presents itself, it must be what's best for us? How do we know? How do we determine when we're settling or when we're truly making the best choice possible?

A TENDENCY TOWARD WANDERLUST

Over the past several years, Jeremy and I have hosted multiple people in our home for months-long stints. As we've established the things our family values, we've found that hospitality is pretty high on our list. And over time, the outpouring of that value has grown to include hosting people though transitional stages of their lives. Mostly our live-ins have been early twentysomethings in a phase of trying to figure out some things in their lives. Jobs ... careers ... relationships. It can take a little while to figure these things out.

We have *loved* having these people in our home. We can sow into them—invest in their lives—and provide a safe place while they're in a period of self-discovery. But something we've noticed about the generation behind us is a tendency toward wanderlust. While I never want to say that we should all just settle, the opposite side of the coin, if we're not careful, can produce a lack of responsibility, rootedness, dependability, and integrity.

God values diligence, faithfulness, and integrity to follow through with our yeses. If we don't train our ears to hear the Lord, we risk becoming a people who are discontent and view any option as settling that isn't constantly fulfilling.

In our own home, we've had a front-row seat the past few years to a generation that is so resolved against settling, they've managed to be perpetually in a state of wandering. In their efforts to find the just right thing, we've seen an inability to settle anywhere. The age to settle into a steady job, get married, and take on responsibility seems to be stretching further and further into what most of us would call adulthood.

Proverbs 19:21 says, "Many are the plans in the mind of a man, but it is the purpose of the LORD that will stand." But how do we determine that purpose? How do we uncover the purpose that God has for us and avoid settling into a plan of our own making?

Settling is when we land anywhere other than the place God has for us. It's not tuning our ears to hear the Lord and follow Him. When we settle, we stop being curious about where we could be going. In addition, we stop being curious about what God could have for us where we are. We embrace complacency in our hearts and in our pursuit of God. Good becomes good enough, and we lose our desire for more of God Himself.

If we want to avoid falling into tired patterns, we must constantly renew our minds by focusing on the things of heaven. All of life is a training ground, and when we settle, we lose our desire to keep moving, to keep pursuing, to keep uncovering new levels of God's goodness for us. In Romans 12:2, Paul put it this way:

Do not be conformed to this world, but be transformed by the renewal of your mind, that by testing you may discern what is the will of God, what is good and acceptable and perfect.

Psalm 37:23–24 reminds us,

The steps of a man are established by the LORD,
    when he delights in his way;
though he fall, he shall not be cast headlong,
    for the LORD upholds his hand.

Whether we step in the wrong direction just to get where we think we want to go or avoid making concrete steps at all, the Lord will uphold us and establish our steps when they are made as we follow Him.

Finding ourselves in a spot different from our expectations doesn't always mean that we've lost our way. When we don't follow God's plan well, sometimes we can wind up having to walk out the rest of a situation we've landed in and miss out on God's best. We may have to walk out "good," when we could have been more fully experiencing His best.

MY STRESS RASH

You may consider this confession too much information (sorry about that), but I wrote part of this book when I had a really hideous rash. It was on my legs, sides, arms, neck, and even on my face. I had this stupid rash because I settled for something less than God's best for me. My doctor told me that the rash was due to stress. Stress that could have been avoided had I done exactly what I'd felt the Lord was telling me to do a while ago.

So I wound up walking out a situation that seemed pretty good for my life. I knew it wasn't God's best, but I did it anyway. I let other people talk me into something that I had to carry to completion for the next several months. I didn't defiantly disobey the Lord; I just allowed voices other than the Lord's to speak loudest in my life.

God gave us the Holy Spirit to help us discern the best way to go. When we measure our opportunities in light of pursuing God and not our own desires, the path becomes clearer. It's in the secret place with the Lord where we learn to know His voice. Where we learn to trust His heart for us. When we sow time with the Father, we learn how to listen and how to hear. Our curiosity to follow God, to discover possibilities previously unimagined, will open doors we never considered and reveal joy in places previously obscured. When the delight of our hearts becomes more about delighting in the Lord, we'll find ourselves much less confused amid all the options and will begin to see triumph in our lives. Rather than settling, we'll become victorious, as the prophet Isaiah wrote:

> If you honor [the ways of the Lord], not going
>> your own ways,
>>> or seeking your own pleasure, or talking
>>>> idly;

> then you shall take delight in the LORD,
> and I will make you ride on the heights of
> the earth. (58:13–14)

After we settle, there's usually not a good way out. And any way out we could find would probably make things worse or hurt other people. When I actually listened to the Lord on the issue, He kinda said, "Here we are. Let's just carry on. It'll be okay."

That's the thing about entering into something that wasn't ever meant for us. Usually we still have to finish the journey despite our reasons for beginning it. The thing about settling is that it doesn't always mean *lowering* our expectations of what we wanted. Instead, we settle for our own expectations of what is good for us rather than what God has that's best.

For example, I wanted to spend more time focusing on my family, so I started homeschooling my boys for the first time and was super-excited about it. But my involvement in other areas required more of me than I would have preferred. All of life puts us in seasons of trade-offs, but I felt I was being forced to trade more than I was willing to.

Writing this book, homeschooling, sowing into my community, and contributing to some philanthropic things on my heart caused my margin to start wearing thin.

First-world problems, I know. But no matter what issues are messing up your margins or creating major stress, it can be easy to miss God's best when things already seem pretty good. For instance, the Lord gave me the opportunity several years ago to be a part of Allume, a Christian-women's blogging and social-media conference and community. I took it over when my friend Sarah Mae passed the torch in 2013. From the first day, I felt that the Lord asked me to simply steward the ministry and carry it until He told me to put it down. *I need you to do this first,* I heard Him say. The community is an incredible space for women, and even some men, who desire to use their influence both online and in real life to make an impact for the kingdom of God. The people involved and the space we've created are really something special.

But before we even finished the conference in 2014, I felt the Lord tell me to lay it down for a bit. I hadn't booked the hotel for 2015 yet, and I was pretty adamant about taking a year off at a minimum. My family needed me, and I just sensed in my spirit that our entire team needed a break, even though everyone appeared energized and excited to keep going.

However, circumstances began to shift around me, and people who truly loved me whispered into my ear that I was making the wrong decision. Some people came alongside and offered to shoulder the responsibility so that I could still be freed up to walk in the things I felt the Lord calling me to do.

Even people who love us and have our best interests in mind can't necessarily hear what the Lord is saying to our hearts. Though I never meant to walk in disobedience, my mind got cloudy as I listened to those around me instead of keeping my ear closely tuned to the Father's heart.

So I agreed to host another conference. A contract was signed with the hotel a month after we closed the 2014 conference, committing us to another year of occupancy. For the record, contracts are meant to be binding. Thus, I still had to walk out the choices I made.

Within weeks of my decision, I began to feel overwhelmed. Where I'd originally planned to invest more in homeschooling, I was rushing through the morning to get the work done so that I could check school off the list by the afternoon. Somehow the work piled higher for Allume than it ever had before. And the afternoons I'd intended to spend with my family turned out being spent in my home office while a babysitter did the things I wanted to do, entertaining my children with Legos and water balloons.

By February I was falling apart. In the midst of all the work and schooling, we sold our house. When it became clear that a planned renovation wasn't going to work out, the stars seemed to align, and the Lord sold our house and found us another one within five days. By the time I'd even begun to warm to the idea of moving, I was waking up in a new room of a really wonderful new house. There is no doubt in my mind that the move was a gift and plan from the Lord, but the move on top of all the work, homeschooling, surgery for my youngest, and a zillion other unexpected stressors just about sent me over the edge.

This could not be Your best, Lord!

I'm fairly sure that while there were plenty of "bests" in the whole lot, the entire scenario wasn't what the Lord wanted me to experience. He knew my son Hudson would need a third eye surgery in 2015. The Lord knew we would move to another house. He knew I'd be writing a book, homeschooling, and trying to keep up my relationships with people near and dear to me.

God knew it all.

In His kindness, He knew my capacity. God knew just how much I could take without falling apart, crying in my closet every day. Had I listened, had I followed more closely, had I not settled for anything other than what I knew He had for me, I wouldn't have written this book covered in a rash.

But, have mercy, God is so kind. Even when something we imagined would be good turns out to run us through the ringer, He still shows up. In His kindness, He doesn't let us fall completely on our faces. He can still give vision, and His purposes will still come to pass. It just may cost us more along the way than He ever wanted us to have to pay.

Let's be clear. Just because something is good, just because it's life giving to others, or even if it's a wonderful ministry doesn't mean it's the *best* thing God has for us right now. When we walk outside of God's best, even "good" can end up feeling like settling. But when we wait on the Lord and trust Him, we experience the best He has to offer us:

> The LORD will guide you continually
>> and satisfy your desire in scorched places
>> and make your bones strong;
> and you shall be like a watered garden,
>> like a spring of water,
>> whose waters do not fail. (Isa. 58:11)

Do we trust God? Do we trust that even when He asks us to wait—to be strong and courageous and wait on Him—that what He has us waiting for is good, or better than good? Do we trust that God truly does want what's *best* for us? And are we willing to turn our ears toward Him to hear what He's speaking to our hearts?

We may not get what we wanted. But the thing we imagined might not be the right fit for our lives. Perhaps God has more than just a hallway of goodness for us. Maybe He has a whole room of greatness waiting for us when we trust and follow Him. We will be like a well-watered garden when we're patient enough to wait on the harvest to come, when we're diligent to seek the heart of God for our lives.

Learning to live curiously often requires us to refuse to settle for "good" so we're ready to receive God's best.

Chapter 9
The Physics of Tension

*Gravity explains the motions of the planets, but it
cannot explain who sets the planets in motion.*

Sir Isaac Newton

Moving is the worst. Okay, so maybe not *the* worst, but in my
opinion it's pretty wretched. I've never met anyone who relishes
packing up an entire life and transplanting, no matter how exciting a new home can feel. Have you?

We bought our house with the intention of renovating it.
Moving wasn't in the plans; we wanted to stay there forever. The
yard was perfect for little boys, teeming with trees, frogs, and
a creek at the back. It was on a cul-de-sac in a quiet, no-outlet
neighborhood with children right around the corner whom we'd
grown to love. Neighbors planted a community garden each
spring, and I looked forward to BLTs made with the Hughes's
tomatoes all year long. In March it looked like the Masters golf

tournament. Azaleas exploded on every bend in the road, and the whole circle drive looked like a watercolor painting.

The community there felt like the community most of America craves. We had lived there seven years. About two weeks before beginning construction, we got news from the bank that the appraisal on the completed project came in way too low. We would be financially underwater if we proceeded with the plans. I cried for two days as I realized that my dreams for our home and life in this perfect-to-us place would come to an end.

Life carries tension: good versus bad, a season for laughing and crying, for living and dying. A season for endings and a season for new beginnings.

Three days after considering that we might move, we saw six houses and settled on one. In all the chaos of our rapid decision making, the Lord had already selected for us exactly what we needed. And just thirty-five days later, we settled in the new house. When I think now about my life and how on earth it would have worked renovating a home I was still planning to live in, my eyes roll to the back of my head. In His kindness, the Lord knew what would have put me in the nuthouse, and He spared me. In the time we sold a house and moved, one of my friends finally chose tile for a master bathroom. How nice for her.

Moving isn't crisis. Choosing tile is *definitely* not crisis. Meeting new neighbors won't destroy us. Making more of an effort to see old ones won't either. Maybe we trade azaleas for hydrangeas and a shower for a tub. Sometimes in our lives, we have major stresses with real problems, but sometimes life's changes just accumulate and cause tension.

NEWTON'S CRADLE

Life doesn't promise that seasons of goodness and hard things won't mingle. In fact, I think tension is something we must learn to embrace lest we fall into a space where we can't see the forest for all the trees.

If we completely give in to the stresses of living, then we might miss the beauty of the gifts God lines up around us. If we let ourselves celebrate only the goodness, then we won't see the ways the Lord wants to speak to our hearts in the midst of the hardships too. So we sit in the middle, with tensions on either side of us swinging back and forth into our lives. Simple versus complicated. Easy and hard. Good, then bad. Healing and hurting. A full life will end up including it all.

When I was in high school, I won the physics award at graduation. Please stop right there, though, before you think too highly of my scientific skill. For real … join me in a good chuckle right quick. You should know that the reasons for my winning that award had more to do with my perseverance in getting extra help than it did for my mastery of Newton's laws. In short, I had no clue what was going on. I was completely inept at physics and was forced to spend nearly every afternoon getting extra help from my teacher.

Shockingly, though, I do remember learning something or other about the laws of motion and momentum. To recount them now, I still have to google "momentum for dummies" or "physics explanations for kids." But the visual for me of Newton's Cradle still illustrates living in tension. While I'm being honest about my lack of sciencey prowess, you should know that I also just had to google "metal ball momentum thingy" to even remember that it was called Newton's Cradle.

But you probably know what I'm talking about too, whether you realize it or not. Maybe you had a teacher with one on his or her desk at some point. It's those five metal balls hanging by cords from a couple of parallel bars. When a ball on the outside hits the three balls in the center, the ball on the opposite side swings out with the same speed and force as the initial dropped ball. So it goes, each side swinging out, hitting the stationary few in the center, and transferring the force to the ball on the opposite side. *Click-clack, click-clack, click-clack* ... back and forth they swing. All the while, the three balls in the middle appear to remain completely still.

Sometimes life can feel sort of like Newton's Cradle. Or you might think life is more like a pendulum swinging high from one side to the other and back again. Imagine roller-coaster highs and lows. You get my drift. It can feel as if things alternate from good to bad and then back to good again.

Why do we find ourselves so shocked by the swings of life? The book of Ecclesiastes foreshadows these changes, but I still feel surprised by the way highs and lows consistently alternate knocking at my door.

> For everything there is a season, and a time for
>   every matter under heaven:
> a time to be born, and a time to die;
> a time to plant, and a time to pluck up what is
>   planted;
> a time to kill, and a time to heal;

a time to break down, and a time to build up;

a time to weep, and a time to laugh;

a time to mourn, and a time to dance;

a time to cast away stones, and a time to
gather stones together;

a time to embrace, and a time to refrain from
embracing;

a time to seek, and a time to lose;

a time to keep, and a time to cast away;

a time to tear, and a time to sew;

a time to keep silence, and a time to speak;

a time to love, and a time to hate;

a time for war, and a time for peace. (3:1–8)

I remember teaching my kids about the events of September 11, 2001. They memorized a synopsis of the terrorist attacks in New York City, and we talked about everything that happened. One day, though, I decided we should watch the news footage of the attack.

We found old *Today* show recordings on YouTube and settled in to watch for probably an hour or more as that day's events unfolded. Al Roker was sharing the weather, as jovial as always. Willard Scott and the Smucker's jam folks were celebrating centennial birthdays the way they do every morning. Crowds cheered outside in Rockefeller Plaza and waved signs to capture their five seconds of television fame. It was such a normal, joyful morning with Matt Lauer, Katie Couric, and the NBC morning-show crew.

Then the disruption came at 8:46 a.m. One New York TV station interrupted a movie commercial with pictures of black smoke billowing from World Trade Center Tower 1.

Click-clack.

The tension of good and evil couldn't have felt more black and white that day. One minute, a time to live … and the next, a time to die.

How do we navigate the drastic black and white we experience in this life? How do we keep from losing ourselves on either side of those extremes? Deeply grieving loss but still finding the capacity to fully celebrate joy. Celebrating triumphs but wholly empathizing with hurt and brokenness. The click-clack of life can shift everything within seconds.

One thing God keeps teaching me about living and functioning in all this tension is that in Him there is stability in the middle of all the highs and lows. Just like Newton's Cradle. In Christ, highs and lows may smack into us from either side. But because of God's faithfulness, they hit a stationary point at our center, where we remain steady. In Christ we find our center, digging deep roots of faith and aligning upward to heaven rather than laterally within the swinging tensions of the earth. When Christ absorbs the click-clack at the center, we're less susceptible to swinging too high or too low.

As children of the Lord, we can live in the center point of Christ. He is the conduit through which all our tensions travel. He channels the energies and absorbs the force. The good influences the bad, and the way we handle the bad fills us with gratefulness as we walk in times of celebration. Learning to navigate tensions and allowing them to make us wiser will instill a depth of character as we enter new circumstances. And knowing how to navigate those tensions breeds a freedom to be more curious about what new things could be in store for us.

A hard experience, when well evaluated and weathered, positions us for growth and the future. We grow from learning how to navigate it all. If we're crushed by every hard experience, we don't have the tools to walk through hard times again. But when we filter all of life through Christ, the tensions make impact, to be certain, but they don't knock us off our center. Curiosity blossoms as we become more confident in our capacity to successfully tackle the swings of life.

LET THIS CUP PASS FROM ME

Hours before His death, Jesus gathered with His disciples in a garden called Gethsemane and said to them,

> "Sit here, while I go over there and pray." And taking with him Peter and the two sons of Zebedee, he began to be sorrowful and troubled. Then he said to them, "My soul is very sorrowful, even to death; remain here, and watch with me." And going a little farther he fell on his face and prayed, saying, "My Father, if it be possible, let this cup pass from me; nevertheless, not as I will, but as you will." (Matt. 26:36–39)

Before Jesus prayed that prayer in the garden, He shared the famous Last Supper with His closest friends on the earth. "Take and eat.... Drink.... Do this to remember Me," He said to the Twelve as He foretold

His death with bread and wine in hand (Luke 22:15–19, paraphrase). And they sat together at that table with sorrowful hearts because of what Jesus said was to come. Celebration and sorrow mingled around the table in that borrowed upper room over a shared Passover meal.

Immediately following the supper, before Jesus even mentioned Peter's impending denial, Scripture says, "And when they had sung a hymn, they went out to the Mount of Olives" (Matt. 26:30).

Bible commentator Matthew Henry asserted that the hymn sung was likely Psalm 113:1–9, a psalm typically sung at the end of Passover celebrations:

> Praise the LORD!
> Praise, O servants of the LORD,
>   praise the name of the LORD!
>
> Blessed be the name of the LORD
>   from this time forth and forevermore!
> From the rising of the sun to its setting,
>   the name of the LORD is to be praised!
>
> The LORD is high above all nations,
>   and his glory above the heavens!
> Who is like the LORD our God,
>   who is seated on high,
> who looks far down
>   on the heavens and the earth?
> He raises the poor from the dust
>   and lifts the needy from the ash heap,

to make them sit with princes,
with the princes of his people.
He gives the barren woman a home,
making her the joyous mother of children.
Praise the LORD!

In his commentary on the whole Bible, Matthew Henry went on to say that "[joy] is not unseasonable, no, not in times of sorrow and suffering; the disciples were in sorrow, and Christ was entering upon his sufferings, and yet they could sing a hymn together. Our spiritual joy should not be interrupted by outward afflictions."[1]

Our spiritual joy should not be interrupted by outward afflictions.

Chew on that one for a minute.

In Christ, our deepest joy doesn't come from our circumstances. In a way, Matthew Henry's assertion is sort of an encouragement. If the situations in our lives aren't what give us the deepest version of joy, then they also aren't able to steal our joy. The joy that sustains us is the joy of the Lord. It's the joy in being called His children, in being redeemed, in being found. No matter the junk we walk through, the hope found in our good God remains.

In the interest of reality, though, let's not pretend we don't actually experience the interruption. September 11 stopped most everyone in their tracks. Interruption to me feels more like a minor distraction, not something that rocks my whole world. The depth of grief from the darkness that we must somehow reconcile in this world can feel awfully earth shattering. It can feel nearly impossible to recover. But when we have a solid center, when our joy doesn't originate from our circumstances, we have the capacity to reach back to that center to have something concrete to hold on to.

"My Father, if it be possible, let this cup pass from me," Jesus pleaded on bended knees in Gethsemane (Matt. 26:39). Sometimes I imagine other things He might have said: "No, Lord.... Please don't make Me do this, Papa. Please don't ask Me to separate from You. Please don't turn Your back on Me. Please, Daddy, I don't want to die. I don't want to be beaten and hung on a cross. I don't want the grief and the sorrow and the weight of all the world for all of time to sit on My shoulders. Let this cup pass from Me."

Even Jesus sat in the tension. His lips loudly praised the goodness of God even as He anticipated the coming betrayal of a friend and the death that awaited Him.

"Not My will, though, but Your will, Father. As You will" (v. 39, paraphrase).

In the midst of our "Seriously, God! What the heck?" kind of circumstances, we have to stay rooted to our center, where the click-clack of good and bad doesn't move us from the knowledge that His will for us is to bring about a hope and a future (see Jer. 29:11). Jesus knew that truth even as He prepared to die. And in releasing our own expectations, we must cling to that truth too.

I wish I could say that curiosity about the Lord increases during these times of tension. But it doesn't always. And you'd probably be annoyed with me if I said that curiosity and faith were as easy and magical as unicorns and rainbows. If I said it was easy, then someday when I go back and reread these words myself, I'd be annoyed with me too. The truth is that in the tension, in the midst of screaming out to God "Seriously?" we don't feel curious. We don't wonder, and we don't want to chase after Him.

At times I've had to force myself to sit before the Lord and open the Scriptures. I've sunk deep into a hot bath till my skin has shriveled, just to wash away my frustration and doubt. Maybe it's just me, but there's something about bubbles and stillness and heat that can recenter us, even if only till the next morning.

Then morning comes, and the enemy reminds us of all the click-clacking back and forth. The roller coaster starts pulling us up a hill and launching us down the other side again. One minute we're bracing for the plunge, with anticipation and excitement, and the next we have knots in our stomachs.

"Praise the name of the Lord!"

"Let this cup pass from me."

The tension is a given; it's how we handle it that defines so much of the way we live.

STRUGGLE IN CELEBRATION

How do you manage the tension when others around you see their happy dreams come to fruition?

My friend Miranda had two children in the time it took me to have one. She eventually bore a total of five in the time I birthed two and lost four. Another friend, Kelley, gave birth to a third child just a month after I finally had my second. Melissa had a baby even after overcoming an initial battle with breast cancer. Joanna lost one and then had three more. Katie was paired with a baby and saw a rapid adoption finalized—all in the time I was aching with loss and unmet longings.

While so many of the stories around me at the time seemed to end with hope happily fulfilled, several of them surely weren't without highs and lows either. But it wasn't only about having a baby. It was just the thing that yielded a very visible outcome for so many people around me. It was such a clear picture for me of the swing. Pregnant with hope and expectation one minute; then everything swings rapidly to loss, crushed dreams, and death. At the end of that nine-month road, you're left holding a baby—or not. I was *not* during that phase of my life, and it seemed everyone else had someone little to hold.

But I loved my friends. And as friends so often do, we made preparations to celebrate these new lives. For more than a year, my circle of friends averaged at least one birth, pregnancy announcement, or baby shower every ten days. The rate of procreation around me rivaled rabbits! For my wounded heart, it was a hard pill to repeatedly swallow, with very little breathing room in between. To keep up with the demand for celebration and make sure our budget aligned with the abundance of blessing all around me, I began sewing baby slings, nursing covers, burp cloths, and changing pads. For almost eighteen months, I pinned and stitched my broken heart as I assembled gifts for new babies popping up everywhere. *What gives, Lord?*

Two babies from my womb now dead, inexplicable infertility, and ovulation cycles religiously tracked defined my formerly enjoyable sex life. All this happened while I was spending hours every week sewing gifts to celebrate the joys of others.

Click-clack. Click-clack.

As I sat in the back rows of baby showers celebrating the miracle of life with my friends, my heart somehow swelled with joy for them and simultaneously shattered with disappointment for myself. The tension was awkward, and I know they all felt it. Celebration and sorrow swaddled the new lives I held in my arms through hospital visits and meals delivered. In the depths of my soul, I was truly happy for my friends. But within those same depths was a dull ache of personal grief and loss that remained.

And so go the seasons …

Click-clack.

Of course, life continued, and more babies were born around me. Eventually I did get pregnant and have our son Hudson. But when that hope fulfilled was followed by more lost pregnancies, I began to realize that I couldn't keep going back to the same well of sorrows, lest I drown in them.

My circumstances couldn't keep defining my hope.

I thought I was going to lose myself during those years. I remember sobbing to my husband, saying, "I don't even know why anyone would want to be my friend. I'm just a broken mess." And I believed it. I couldn't seem to get my bearings on my life or my emotions. I went to see a counselor, engaged in things I enjoyed, and tried to find the pieces of myself that I thought I'd lost.

Somewhere in the muck that clung tightly around my weighted spirit, I remembered the faithfulness of God.

Great is Thy faithfulness, O God my Father,
There is no shadow of turning with Thee;
Thou changest not, Thy compassions, they fail not
As Thou hast been Thou forever wilt be.[2]

Great is Thy faithfulness. Even though it didn't feel true to me at the time, I clung to the promise of the company of God with me in my sorrow. I joined a book study with some women from our church, and we read *The Supernatural Power of a Transformed Mind* by Bill Johnson. That book rocked my world! I realized that I was living under the power of a conformed mind trapped in the pattern of the world (see Rom. 12:2) and that God, in His goodness and faithfulness, wanted to make me new again. He wanted to transform my mind to hold on to His promises instead of allowing the circumstances around me to set the temperature of my life.

I didn't even know how to do that—to reset the temperature of my boiler-room life. Somewhere in that study, even though I felt like I was sitting in a sauna, it was as if I'd found a tiny hole in a wall to breathe cool air. I began to find refreshment in the promises of God for me, and I clung to them with desperation for new hope.

Around that time I learned about praying the opposite (see the end of chapter 3 for a refresher). I began to apply the truth of God to the wild pendulum swinging of my life. Instead of focusing on all the things that felt as if they were eating me alive, I returned to a steadiness found in the faithfulness of God, and my curiosity was refreshed.

I remember one time having a sort of epiphany about Psalm 23, which for most of my life, I would have said was an elementary understanding. One minute David was talking about God leading him to green pastures and still, soul-restoring waters. But on the same walk with the Lord, David also passed through the aptly named valley of the shadow of death. David didn't freak out when the scenery changed; he just kept moving forward.

"I will fear no evil, for you are with me" (v. 4). I wonder how that feels to be strolling along a stream, noting the stillness of the waters, the calm of the space, the verdant grass around you, and then to find yourself eyes wide open in the valley of the shadow of DEATH!

Click-clack, right?

In 2 Corinthians 5, the apostle Paul talked about walking by faith and not by sight. I guess I always sort of thought it just meant to be blind in our trust. Ignorance is bliss, and the less we know, the more faithful we can be, right? Maybe so … but that's the childlike bit, huh? Then one day I realized that walking by faith doesn't mean that we walk blind through the valley of the shadow of death. It occurred to me, perhaps for the first time, that walking by faith isn't living in ignorance or blinded to the hardships around us. Instead, it means facing the hardships head-on, seeing them and choosing to believe that because the Lord is with us, we don't have to fear the evil.

BEARS KILL STUFF

The year we took our first family trip to Glacier National Park in Montana (the trip when I took the helicopter ride I mentioned earlier), we met up with a dear old friend and his family. One day we went hiking on the eastern side of the park—four adults with five children under the age of eight. We remained relatively close together, being sure to make reasonable amounts of noise along the way because of … *grizzly bears*.

You may remember the quote I tossed in for your laughing pleasure earlier: "What doesn't kill you makes you stronger, except bears ... because bears will kill you!" Yeah, I was thinking about bears as we meandered in fields of wildflowers and pointed at little groundhogs popping out of holes to enjoy a snack on top of a sunny rock. We walked carefully across a shallow river, glistening with smooth pebbles just inches beneath the surface, and continued along the path, where a stream ran directly beside our trail.

Stopping to point out flowers, animals, and interesting tidbits along the way, we slowly but surely made our way along the three-mile route that would end at a lake. It was glorious, peaceful, and stunning as we walked through those green pastures along still waters.

Then I looked down to notice a small tuft of thick white fur on the bank about five feet from me. "Oh, look, guys, a mountain goat must be shedding. Look at this bit of its fur!" The discovery was so delightful for us all! We paused for a moment and then continued to walk. Within just a few more steps, there was another tuft of fur, and then another that was more a chunk of fur. My eyes lifted along the bank of the stream opposite where we were walking, within mere feet of our trail, to see that the entire hillside was littered with various pieces of what had once been a mountain goat. Sticks and small saplings had been snapped off in what appeared to be a frenzied mess. Then we saw a few bony remains of the goat in a pile at the top of the small bank.

I felt my stomach drop into my shoes, and my heart began to beat rapidly. "What in the world? Shut up ... that is *not* from a ... oh, my gracious ... please tell me ... NOOO!

"Kids, all of you get back here! You cannot walk ahead of us *at all*!"

We were literally standing in a valley of the shadow of *very recent* death. As in, the park ranger told us later that the mess we saw hadn't been there just a few hours before.

Forget it, Psalm 23! I don't even want to hear it! I feared that valley right then, y'all, because … um … GRIZZLY BEARS! I feared the heck out of that valley. All the way to the lake and back, I feared that valley like it was my job.

Maybe that doesn't give me a right to talk … because I *feared*. I mean, deep in my bones, shaking in my boots, throwing up a little in my mouth right then FEARED that valley. Now, I'm not advocating that we go all Siegfried and Roy and tempt fate with a lack of healthy fear. But we can't allow our fear to cripple our faith walk, as we talked about before.

In the Psalms, David was talking about learning to see the goodness of the Lord as well as taking full account of the valley around us. We fully celebrate the peaceful calm of still waters. But we also feel the chill in our bones when death scatters remains of the living on a hillside around us. We walk the seasons of change, and to keep from being defined by the things around us, we find constant stability rooted at the center of Christ:

> Your steadfast love is before my eyes,
>   and I walk in your faithfulness. (Ps. 26:3)

> I the LORD do not change; therefore you, O children of Jacob, are not consumed. (Mal. 3:6)

God is still good. He doesn't change. The presence of God is constant, and though we wish life tarried in green pastures forever, we have to know that in His goodness, the Lord won't allow us to be consumed or leave us to weather the rough blows of seasonal change alone. The psalmist proclaimed,

> Of old [God] laid the foundation of the earth,
>> and the heavens are the work of your
>> hands.
> They will perish, but you will remain;
>> they will all wear out like a garment.
> You will change them like a robe, and they
>> will pass away,
> but you are the same, and your years have
>> no end. (102:25–27)

> The counsel of the LORD stands forever,
>> the plans of his heart to all generations.
>> (33:11)

The wild swings from sorrow to celebration will never cease, and we must walk, eyes wide open, focused on the faithfulness of our good God to find our constant center.

Click … Great is Thy faithfulness … *clack* … You do not change.

Click … You are good … *clack* … I will not be consumed.

Just like Newton's Cradle, all the forces in our lives come to rest at the center.

Chapter 10

When We Carry Heavy Things

*There's a very good chance you'll meet things that scare you
right out of your pants ... down the road between hither and
yon ... can scare you so much you won't want to go on.*

Dr. Seuss, *Oh, the Places You'll Go!*

An army of dear friends circled the wooden sleigh bed as my friend Melissa sat propped up against quilted pillows. We gathered around her to do battle in the heavenlies. We held hands and spoke words uttered from the depths of souls weary from a long fight. The room filled with "the tongues of men and of angels" (1 Cor. 13:1). Nine of us stood around Melissa that day, contending for a miracle.

"I just can't seem to get over this cough," she told us two summers earlier while sitting at the sturdy picnic tables of Pittman Park.

"It's so frustrating. This dang bronchitis just won't go away!"

By fall we learned that what doctors had labeled as bronchitis and pneumonia was in fact the cancer that had once stolen a breast and was now coming back for a lung. Same strain, new location.

Time lines get fuzzy when battles are waged over years. But by the time Melissa was beginning chemo and radiation, our friend group had already created meal and childcare schedules with no end date. For two years we cooked healthy foods to strengthen her weakening body. We alternated care for three children whose mommy was too weak from strong medicines that were simultaneously saving and breaking down her system. And we prayed like never before. All of us had witnessed miracles, and we claimed one for her too. When one of us would falter in big faith, the others would reinforce our foundations time and again with the promises of our miraculous God throughout Scripture. We held one another up as we held Melissa up.

My God had covered the moon. Baby Cohen breathed, and I believed that Melissa would keep breathing.

Melissa was always spunky. She was stylish, smart, quick witted, and honest. She had her own way, and she knew who she was. First and foremost, she was a daughter of the Most High God. She'd been a wife to Brad for nearly twenty years. She was mommy to her eight-year-old boy and her two miracle girls, ages four and two. Doctors told her she couldn't have children after the cancer came the first time. But she believed the God of creation over their diagnosis and went on to have both of her girls.

Melissa was a piece of work, and we loved her like a sister.

God is so good to give us friends like that. To show us miracles like Melissa's girls. To fill our lives with His goodness.

Sometimes, though, life just gets really heavy. Sometimes you're taking meals to your friend's family and caring for her kids. She's forty, has a husband and three little ones, and is dying of cancer. You've prayed for years, but she still dies.

You've prayed, but she *still* dies.

The day we gathered for Melissa's funeral, death hung in the air, permeating the black-clothed mourners scattered around the room. But her friends planned in advance the way we wanted to remember her. Like fish out of water, we walked into her funeral all dressed up for Melissa. We wore our most bohemian outfits, most embroidered tops, coolest shoes, funkiest hair, and most put-together makeup, and we honored the heck out of the friend she was to us. We celebrated the person she was and the life she lived.

Death can't rob us of the life we leave. Death can't rob us of the life we give. Death can't rob us of the redemption we call ours because of a man named Jesus who rose from the dead. God promises,

> When you are in tribulation, and all these things come upon you in the latter days, you will return to the LORD your God and obey his voice. For the LORD your God is a merciful God. He will not leave you or destroy you or forget the covenant with your fathers that he swore to them. (Deut. 4:30–31)

Life is hard. Sometimes we watch the world crumble around the people we love. Other times the crumbling world is our own. Sometimes the wretched happens, and we have to reconcile that.

And sometimes we can't. We cannot live our lives curiously after God when we spin our wheels trying to reconcile the irreconcilable.

Sometimes we just can't.

We weren't even supposed to know the difference between good and evil. We weren't ever meant to see death versus life. When Adam and Eve ate the forbidden fruit in the garden, they tasted something God never wanted them to know about in the first place. Eating from the Tree of Knowledge of Good and Evil opened their eyes to the difference between the two. As I mentioned early on, God removed them from the garden before they had a chance to get into more trouble with other fruits beyond their capacity. Thanks, Adam and Eve. We weren't supposed to know. We aren't always meant to understand.

WRESTLING WITH THE SCRIPTURES

We often turn to the Scriptures in search of wisdom and encouragement. However, we can't forget that they are also ripe with the narrative of disappointment and brokenness. There's enough personal disaster in the Bible to spawn Lifetime original movies forever: Job; Leah; Bathsheba; Tamar; Mary, the mother of Jesus; and hundreds more. Thank you, Genesis through Revelation, for all the drama.

Job is the obvious character to illustrate massive loss and disappointment. He was a wealthy father of many, who lost finances and family. His friends turned on him, and God Himself gave Job a lecture on His sovereignty that lasted for chapters. Job's is a tale of drastic biblical woe and loss that none can forget.

But what about Leah—an unsightly, scorned, and despised woman who married and slept with her sister's fiancé? Or Rachel, who was betrayed by her father and lost her beloved to her own sister? And when she finally did marry him, she was unable to conceive. One woman loved and barren, the other loathed and fertile. I can hardly stand the tension.

Can you even imagine how it must have felt to be Bathsheba? One day you're taking a bath, and shortly afterward, you're summoned by a king for his sexual pleasure. And because you actually please the king, because he thinks you're beautiful, he murders the husband you love and takes you as his own. You've done what was required of you, and the punishment of illness and death intended for the king falls on your firstborn son instead. Bathsheba paid the price for someone else's disobedience.

In 2 Samuel, the incident where King David's son Amnon violated his sister, Tamar, is nothing short of gut wrenching and despicable. Tricked into caring for someone she believed was an ill sibling, she was violently raped and then cast into the streets with disdain. Her story makes my stomach churn. A cherished sibling counseled her not to "take this to heart" (13:20), and she lived the rest of her life a desolate woman. Where is the justice for Tamar, God? Where is Your mercy and kindness, Lord?

Or to be Mary, the mother of Jesus—a child bride inexplicably pregnant who gave birth in the midst of livestock on the floor of a dank cave. A woman who raised a child she couldn't understand, who was worried to death when, as a boy, He stayed behind in a town just to listen to great teachers. A woman who stood at the foot of a bloodied cross, watching her Son pierced with nails and crowned with mocking thorns to pay for crimes He didn't commit.

How do we make sense of the senseless? How do we reconcile the irreconcilable? How do we carry the heavy things and not break our backs in the process?

There are things in this world that won't make sense this side of heaven. In fact, there will be things in this world that we'll never be able to wrap our finite minds around.

Why do bad things happen to good people? Why is there war? Why all the brokenness? Where are You in it all, God? Are You even there? Do You even see? Why don't You do something? Do something!

I don't know a soul who hasn't wrestled with these questions at some point or another. Maybe you're still wrestling.

Wrestling has been happening since the genesis of creation. And woundedness from those struggles has as well. In Genesis we read that

> Jacob was left alone. And a man wrestled with him until the breaking of the day. When the man saw that he did not prevail against Jacob, he touched his hip socket, and Jacob's hip was put out of joint as he wrestled with him. Then he said, "Let me go, for the day has broken." But Jacob said, "I will not let you go unless you bless me." And he said to him, "What is your name?" And he said, "Jacob." Then he said, "Your name shall no longer be called Jacob, but Israel, for you have striven with God and with men, and have prevailed." (32:24–28)

Wrestling just for the sake of wrestling will wound us and those around us. The longer we wrestle, the more we will continue to wound ourselves and others. Fighting to understand things that are beyond our understanding—well, that can eat us alive. Fights can leave scars, but our scars cannot be what define us. We have to learn to wrestle for a purpose. And, like Jacob, we have to wrestle until we receive God's blessing.

What does it look like to wrestle well with God? Not turning away or running away, but just an all-out roll-on-the-ground-because-I-can't-seem-to-figure-it-out-but-have-to-get-back-close-to-Him wrestle.

It's not a piddly thumb wrestle. And it's not a looks-fancy-but-is-really-fake-blood WWE-style wrestle either. It's like a little boy wrestling with his dad. He's learning how to fight, but he'll never learn how to fight well if he doesn't learn how to wrestle well first. We never learn how to overcome if we don't hang in till the end.

My boys love to wrestle with their dad. As soon as he walks in the door, both of my little guys are nagging him for a wrestle. Tossing on the ground, rolling around, pinning, squishing, squeezing, and sometimes even not-so-comfortable wrestling. In our house, we call it Domination. And Daddy always wins. But my boys still love to play it. The more they play it, the better they get at it, and someday they'll dominate their dad. They'll come out on top in a wrestle because they will have learned how to do it well. They keep at it for the blessing.

It's okay to wrestle when you wrestle well, my friend.

SETTING THE CAPTIVES FREE

We live in a fallen world. But God is bigger than all of it, and He will restore what is broken. We can have confidence in that truth because we know who God is and who He says we are. Knowing the character of God gives us hope and an anchor to cling to in the storms of life:

> People swear by something greater than themselves, and in all their disputes an oath is final for confirmation. So when God desired to show more convincingly to the heirs of the promise the unchangeable character of his purpose, he guaranteed it with an oath, so that by two unchangeable things, in which it is impossible for God to lie, we who have fled for refuge might have strong encouragement to *hold fast to the hope set before us*. We have this as a sure and steadfast anchor of the soul, a hope that enters into the inner place behind the curtain, where Jesus has gone as a forerunner on our behalf. (Heb. 6:16–20)

Restoration doesn't mean that God is going to fix something to look exactly the same way it did before it was broken. It doesn't mean that the redeemed outcome is a delivery of a fulfilled dream that shattered either. But it does mean that when you know that God is good and that He creates life from the ashes, there is redemption to be found.

Jesus lived as a forerunner in our behalf. The entire story of the cross is that of brokenness and redemption. It's the story of life after death, of old being made new. It's beauty from ashes and pain to restoration.

Things may not always work out in our lives in a way that feels to us like the kind of justice we would have chosen. But God is good, and He is called Redeemer.

You have to decide. Do you believe that God can redeem whatever brokenness is in your life? Do you believe that He is who He says He is? Do you know that Jesus came and died just for you? Because He did. Just for you. Just to redeem your brokenness. Just to carry your heavy things.

He broke … for you. He carried two trees bound together through a town that betrayed Him and stood willingly as His back was shredded with whips of hatred. Brow bloodied by thorns that mocked, hands and feet pierced through, and then He hung. All the weight of a man increased infinitely by all the sins of the world … hanging, bearing down, exerting all that is still heavy on His body pressed hard against a wooden cross. It was all so heavy.

He bore it for us. He bore it for you. Then He died from the weight of it all … the crushing, death-inducing heaviness of the whole world for all of time.

But He didn't stay dead. He rose from the grave. Jesus came back to life. He absorbed those burdens, the weight, the brokenness, the pain, and He got up.

He got up so that you can too.

Get up from what is holding you down. Cast off the heavy things onto the cross, over and over if you have to. That's what it's for. That's who Jesus is, and that's why He came to take your heavy things and breathe new life into the deadened spaces of your soul. He takes the weight and replaces it with redemption. He lifts the burden and shares the yoke so that you can shed the shackles of brokenness and walk softly, walk in faith, walk in curiosity after Him.

Black and white is always hard. We like gray because it gives us an in-between, some flex, and it doesn't require us to make specific decisions. But when we carry heavy things, we have to decide if we will carry the heaviness ourselves or allow the Lord to shoulder the weight.

Is God who He says He is or not? Did Jesus mean *me* when He said that He came to set the captives free? Did He mean you? What did He mean when He spoke these words?

> The Spirit of the Lord is upon me,
>   because he has anointed me
>   to proclaim good news to the poor.
> He has sent me to proclaim liberty to the
>   captives
>   and recovering of sight to the blind,
>   to set at liberty those who are oppressed.
>   (Luke 4:18)

This life will bring the heavy. Death is inevitable. Broken people break things … sometimes other people. We can't avoid pain, but we don't want to be people who are defined by our pain more than we're defined by the redemption of it.

You are more than a survivor!

YOU ARE NOT YOUR BROKENNESS

"Logan, we are exactly the same. I've been so looking forward to meeting you! We just have *so much* in common," the woman said cheerfully, stretching out her arm to hand me her business card.

I glanced down at the smiling face printed on the glossy rectangle in my hand and read the words underneath her name. "Mother of three, one died, still surviving," the card said.

Before I even knew it, the words escaped my mouth: "It's so nice to meet you. But we aren't the same, you and I. You are completely defining yourself by the things that broke you. It's part of your story, but you aren't your brokenness."

I could hardly believe the words as they came out of my mouth. *For crying out loud, Logan, think before you speak.* What a jerk! It sounded so harsh, even if I believed every word.

Startled, she looked at me and said, "I just don't want to forget. I'm afraid if I move on, I'll forget."

"You are not your brokenness. The sum of all you are isn't wrapped up in the things that break you most. The sum of you is walking out of those things and being changed and redeemed from the broken, not defined by the pain. You are more than the pain you've borne, and you have redemption to offer your family and the world. Growth isn't forgetting; it's overcoming the pain and choosing to live out the redemption of your own story."

Through tears she said, "You're right. I guess I hadn't ever thought about it that way."

We talked for a long time about living for the people in our lives instead of allowing the dead to rob us of life. It was a deep conversation that lasted well over an hour … because heavy things take a while to unpack. They weigh a lot and deserve time and investment (more than we could even give that day). We don't overcome pain in an instant. We fear that finding peace and resolution may require us to believe that what happened will be forgotten. But in a fallen world, when an enemy steals, it's okay to call that brokenness what it is. We sow seeds of life and health. For those seeds to grow into a harvest, it takes a full season. Galatians says,

> Whatever one sows, that will he also reap. For the one who sows to his own flesh will from the flesh reap corruption, but the one who sows to the Spirit will from the Spirit reap eternal life. And let us not grow weary of doing good, for in due season we will reap, if we do not give up. (6:7–9)

In his book *Secrets of the Secret Place* (a favorite of mine), Bob Sorge said, "What we sow today will require an entire season of growth before the results are manifest."[1] Here's the thing, though. We will carry heavy things. Some people carry more heavy than others, and I don't dare minimize the grief and wretched circumstances many have walked through. No matter our pain, though, no matter the magnitude of grief or wrong we hold, the solution is the same. The pace may look different, but the solution is the same.

Walk toward the cross. Seek out the redemptive works along the way. Pay attention to the joys around you and fight hard for the blessing. Stay curious. You're carrying heavy things, and some seasons may last longer than others. But in due season, if you don't grow weary of doing good, if you don't allow the brokenness to overtake you, you'll reap a harvest. Wrestle to see blessing. Look hard to find redemption. Every little victory is still a victory. Celebrate those steps. When you stumble and fall, get up again.

We aren't the walking dead. We're the walking redeemed people of a living Jesus. Because of Christ, we aren't the living dead; we have access to living even though we were formerly dead.

Lauren grew up in an abusive household. Her father sexually abused her from the time she was young. Her mother was unaware of the abuse, and her sisters didn't know what happened just down the hall from them until they were grown. The horror Lauren endured in a place that should have been safe marked her life and marriage for a long time.

But she kept wrestling. She kept pursuing God, searching the Scriptures to prove to herself that the Father of Abraham wasn't the same as the father of her youth. Over time and through the wise counsel of others, the hardness in her heart softened, and she embraced the redemption God had for her. Her marriage moved into a healthy place as the love of a good and caring Father repaired her heart.

Today Lauren is one of my favorite people. Her zeal for life and her energy are contagious. She is awesome! The Lord has given her a passion to pour out her life in children's ministry, where she shares the God she discovered in her own wrestle. Where she was once broken, she now brings life to others. Rather than looking back at the life she lived as a survivor, she now looks forward to the life that is to come as a conqueror.

In the Bible, Job lost everything. He lost his children, his wealth, his friends, and his health. He was standing on the edge of death. At times he felt as if he had no hope and begged for reprieve. When it didn't come, he blamed God for his suffering, a thing God did in fact allow.

I don't know why God allowed those terrible things to happen to Job—or to you. But I do know that as Job remained faithful to seek the Lord despite his circumstances, he endured and overcame. "Though he slay me," Job declared, "I will hope in him; yet I will argue my ways to his face" (13:15).

In his anguish, Job cried out,

> Oh that my words were written!
>> Oh that they were inscribed in a book!
> Oh that with an iron pen and lead
>> they were engraved in the rock forever!
> For I know that my Redeemer lives,
>> and at the last he will stand upon the
>> earth.
> And after my skin has been thus destroyed,
>> yet in my flesh I shall see God.
>> (19:23–26)

It's okay to be angry when we endure hard things. But we have to take that anger to the Lord. To argue our case before Him. To scream and yell and ask why. And if we don't get an answer, then we fall into the arms of the One we can trust to redeem it all somehow. He will redeem it somehow.

REDEEMING CURIOSITY

The Lord blessed the latter days of Job's life even more than the years before all his suffering and loss. He went on to have ten more children. He gained twice the fortune he had before. The final sentence of the book of Job says, "And Job died, an old man, and full of days" (42:17). Full of days. The days that were lost, Job never got back. The children who died stayed buried in the ground. But Job died an old man, *full* of days.

God will restore.

As we saw earlier in the stories of Rachel and Leah, life was always hard for these sisters. They got lost along the way. Leah bore Jacob six sons and made no bones about taunting her sister with that fact. They got into what appeared to be nothing less than a competition to bear children. They even gave Jacob their slaves to claim offspring as their own. But Rachel was most loved and eventually bore Jacob two sons. One of those sons was Joseph, who ultimately saved his family from famine after his brothers traded him as a slave. The story of Joseph in itself offers redemption from horrific pain.

Rachel and Leah bore the twelve tribes of Israel. They were the mothers of nations. Jacob became wealthy, despite the fact that his father-in-law repeatedly cheated him, and the blessing of the Lord was on his household. I don't know what bits along the way felt redeeming to Rachel and Leah, but I do know that now we see the whole story. We see the redemptive work, and it serves as a testimony to us.

God is in the business of redemption.

Bathsheba went on to become the mother of Solomon. And when another of David's sons sought to proclaim himself king, she had the authority to ask David to award the throne to Solomon. She never got back the husband she lost or the child who died for David's sin. She never saw those lives restored, but her son Solomon went on to become a king of great wisdom, wealth, and power. What Bathsheba gained in the end never replaced what she lost, but there was goodness and beauty and even the promotion of her bloodline.

Second Samuel tells us that after her rape and rejection, Tamar went on to live a desolate life in the house of her brother Absalom. He eventually waged a war in her behalf and killed the perpetrator, Amnon. The wrongs done to her were avenged, but the story doesn't exactly end with a flowery tale of recovery. She was vindicated and her dignity was restored. Yet we're left with the tension of not knowing what happened beyond a life of apparent desolation. She was a daughter of the king and was cared for all her days. While the story may not end with warm fuzzies, it does seal shut with justice.

Justice may be a part of our redemptive stories. But even if it's not, we know that we still dwell in the house of the King, who loves us and will care for us.

And Mary, the mother of Jesus? The mother of *Jesus*. Her Son bled and died for the sins of the world. And while I can't imagine that the ache of loss lessened even after her Son ascended alive to heaven, the end of her story is the same ending for all of ours. And it's still redeeming stories thousands of years later. Her ache may have always remained, but her redemption is still changing stories today.

Restoration doesn't always mean we'll see things replaced that have been lost. Even when fires burn whole forests, though, new life emerges from the fertile, ash-covered ground. Redemption exchanges that which is broken for wholeness. While Lauren didn't see justice come to her father, the things she overcame give her authority to bring the hope of a redeemed testimony to others. Though we may want to see justice done for wrongs committed, God may use our triumphs to bear hope instead.

Like the brokenness that threads through story after story in Scripture, we may never see a redemption that satisfies our unanswered questions. We have to be able to make peace with that. We have to make peace with knowing that perhaps our broken stories will be redeemed through our children or grandchildren. My broken story may be redeemed through the authority I'm given to breathe life into other people's stories.

The brokenness of babies lost is part of my story, but it isn't who I am. It isn't the totality of me. However, since this road is the one I have walked, God has given me a holy passion to love well the daughters of heaven. I have a unique understanding and compassion now, and because of that, new ministry and life grow from those scorched places. It's not what I wanted. It doesn't erase the ache of loss. But I'd be a fool to miss the blessings that are still around and meant for me. My story is still unfolding. I don't know where it will take me, but I'm curious to see what may be in store.

As for my friend Melissa who died, all of us who loved her are still working to see more pieces of redemption in her story. The days of her life still testify even after her death. The friendships sealed through shared hardship are strong. I learned how to pray and stand in faith and believe bigger than I ever thought possible. Just because the end wasn't what I had hoped or wanted, to lose the capacity to believe that big would have been nothing short of tragic. My faith capacity was expanded in Melissa's behalf, and I don't want to lose that just because I lost her. The God I believed could save her is still the same. He is still the same.

Sometimes we may not be able to fix what's broken. But that brokenness cannot overcome us and define who we are or how we walk. We have to make peace with not knowing and not understanding. We can't lose the capacity to walk curiously after the Lord just because we can't make sense of everything that happens in a broken world. Nothing can separate us from the love of God, and "in all these things we are more than conquerors" (Rom. 8:37).

Hope and curiosity are still for us. And when we carry heavy things, we have to believe that the redemptive work of the cross can and will be redemption enough. In the end God always wins. He always restores. He always redeems. In His kindness, He allows us to take baby steps to live a fully engaged life. The process is gentle but still requires us to diligently follow and curiously pursue the Lord, even when we don't feel like it. If we want to uncover increased possibility for our lives, we must cultivate the soil of our souls to prepare them for harvest.

PART 3

A Curious Pursuit
of Hope

Chapter 11
Tiny Yeses

*Do the difficult things while they are easy and do
the great things while they are small. A journey of a
thousand miles must begin with a single step.*

Lao Tzu

The topic of wild obedience was first presented to me as the theme of
a conference at which I had the privilege of speaking. I hadn't given
much thought to that pairing of words before. But the concept really
hit me when I taught a group of women from my church.

A number of younger women began asking to learn from those
of us who were a few years ahead of them. My friend Lindsey had the
idea of launching a series of meetings with simple yet practical-living
topics. The goal was pretty basic stuff, such as older women training
younger ones and not ever discounting what we could learn from
them in return. The group rotated meetings in different homes and
began covering topics ranging from sewing on a button to folding a
fitted sheet, hosting a dinner party, and so on.

I've been passionate for years about hospitality and inviting people into my home, so I began getting excited about hosting the women for my week of teaching. Magic happens around tables where walls come down and lives are exchanged. I was thrilled to teach these younger women a few tips and tricks to make it feel easier to host people in their own homes.

The agenda for our meeting was to share hints on how to set a table and shop your own home to create centerpieces, as well as hands-on instruction on making a few favorite recipes for when company comes over. I was prepared for the whole thing to be fun. But I was surprised to discover that the younger women were like sponges. They seemed desperate to learn, and many had never learned anything about hospitality from their mothers or other women in their lives. (As a total aside, please get outside your comfort zone and sow into women who are a few steps of life behind you. They're desperate for it!)

After teaching the younger ladies how to make flank steak, shrimp and grits, roasted veggies, and a fancy salad, I sat down with them to share the meal and answer questions. At one point a single gal expressed her concern about living in a small townhome. She didn't have proper dishes, much less a dining room or random accessories to create a bohemian, Anthropologie-style vignette in the center of her table.

"I don't have a pretty space like this, or even real dishes," she worried aloud.

Immediately the Lord quickened my spirit to affirm her by saying that what God wants most are our yeses of obedience, not perfect execution. Then I remembered a story I didn't even realize was still tucked back in my psyche.

It was my freshman year at Furman University, and the assignment was a project for the third-level Spanish class I was taking. All students had to come up with something traditionally Spanish to share with the entire class. It could be anything.

I've always loved to cook, so I decided to make a flan. In case you're not flan proficient, it's a relatively complicated egg custard with caramelized sugar on the top. Not your beginner sort of recipe. I might have been in over my head.

I lived in a dorm but figured that as long as I was going to be cooking something in our tiny kitchen, I might as well double up and do something else fun. Because what are two flans when you're already making one?

For the life of me, I couldn't tell you what else I made besides that flan. I do remember roping in a couple of my hall mates for the plan to host a real dinner party. In the dorm kitchen. Because, you know, I was going to be making flan anyway.

Over the years I've learned to create a lovely setting for a dinner party. But a freshman dorm kitchen doesn't exactly come stocked with lovelies or high-functioning appliances. Scratchy, hard cushions crammed into ugly wooden chairs aren't exactly a blank canvas for beauty. Tucked into the corner of the Blackwell Hall kitchen sat a small round table for five that I'm sure had years' worth of chewed gum lurking beneath. Sometimes, though, you've just gotta make do with what you've got.

What mattered was that we used what we had. We didn't wait until a circumstance seemed perfect to begin. We brought what one could only describe as our eighteen-year-old culinary A game to the table.

To this day, when I look back on it, I can still see Lindsay, Laura, Tim, Matt, and Kevin around that table, eating Spanish flan and laughing over dinner … in the dormitory kitchen.

Annie Dillard said, "How we spend our days is … how we spend our life."[1] As far as I can tell, the way we spend or pass anything boils down to a matter of stewardship. If this life has only so many days, then how we spend each day and each moment, as well as how we make each decision, can become a question of stewardship. How are we stewarding the lives we're living? Because the way we steward our moments along the way might very well be a divine setup for things to come. One moment might very well be a tiny step that eventually leads to bigger moves into things we wouldn't have been curious enough to consider before. Tiny yeses are baby steps to uncover deeper curiosity within us. If a curious faith is a mobile one, then stewarding our moments well and saying tiny yeses along the way are part of that forward mobility.

WILD OBEDIENCE

One day I posted on Facebook looking for suggestions for devotionals to do with my kids for our first year joining the ranks of homeschoolers. My friend Brooke shared with me that her boys have really enjoyed learning about different missionaries. She said the stories engaged their curious minds with the notion of brave and daring possibilities. The stories of old tickled their interest in some of the places people can go, the opportunities they can have, and the adventures that can define their lives when they seek the Lord.

After Brooke's recommendation, I began to recall people like Jim and Elisabeth Elliot, Corrie ten Boom, and George Müller. I realized that their testimonies remind us of real people whose stewardship became legendary. History is full of regular people whose wild obedience led them into lives they likely had never imagined for themselves.

The thing is, though, no one ever just *arrives* at a life that may look like an epic success or adventure. No one just waltzes into hard things out of nowhere. When we begin to see pieces of life stories that are inspiring, those people likely put in the hard work and the baby steps of obedience along the way. By the time we see something inspiring in their stories, there have probably been a zillion steps along the way that prepared those people for the roles they walk in now.

Perhaps along the way, some steps may look like wild obedience from the outside looking in. But in reality, walking in obedience and operating in wisdom become the least wild things we can ever do.

If we think of the word *wild* as defined by Webster, we may imagine something "unruly, unrestrained, and undisciplined." But when we're talking about wildness in terms of obedience, the only thing that becomes truly unruly is when we walk outside of it. Someone's "wild" story may simply be the next yes for that person in a long series of obedient small steps.

One of my dearest friends, Laura Parker, is currently living what many would call a pretty wild story. Laura and her husband, Matt, founded an incredible organization called the Exodus Road, which runs covert operations in Southeast Asia to rescue young girls from sex trafficking. We're talking pen-camera undercover agents, stings on brothels, and bars-selling-underage-girls-for-sex kind of stuff. It's a story of a former youth pastor now wearing spy gear and working with local authorities in strip clubs and bars in Asia to bust down doors and rescue little girls from horrific lives. It's pretty insane stuff.

To many people looking in from the outside, Matt and Laura's story stands out as one of wild obedience. The Parkers moved to Asia with three young children so they could be closer to the operatives and programs they're running. Let's not even get started on a wife sending her husband into strip clubs night after night to find little girls to rescue! What the Parkers do is gritty and hard and out of obedience to what the Lord has enabled them to do.

But the thing is, I've known Laura since we were six. Laura was having quiet times with the Lord pretty much as soon as she could read. She was going on mission trips as a teenager and has been loving people well as long as I can remember. Laura was voted the homecoming queen in high school not because she was the center of attention but because everyone loved her. Everyone loved her because she loved everyone. She has been faithful to the things the Lord has asked of her and has persevered through the hard things. She's not perfect. She gets frustrated on hard days, yells at her kids, and loses her cool like we all do. But she has put in the time along the way. Laura has stewarded the small steps that lead to the hard steps. By the time the Lord first asked her to send her husband into a brothel to rescue little girls, it was the next right step in a series of them. It was simply the next right thing to do to be obedient.

Think about your own life. Can you identify some little steps along the way that have led you to the place you are now? Imagine if you had taken just a few steps differently. How could that have redirected your course? How have your tiny yeses of obedience moved you in directions you never would have gone had they required big answers to big questions? Maybe you feel stuck. Think in baby steps. What small things can you change that can begin to shift your perspective and maybe even your circumstances?

I'm not a runner. I've tried ... goodness knows I've tried. But try as I might, it's still not something that arrests my soul in fireworks of delight. We all probably have friends who are runners, some who have even been so insane as to run marathons. Maybe you're one of those weird people? Just kidding. I'm jealous of your brand of awesome.

I've noticed some things about running a marathon. No person just wakes up one morning and pounds out 26.2 miles. For someone like me, it would begin with figuring out how to run just one mile ... then two ... then four ... and so on. It's building up and adding on. Even though I hear that 26.2 miles kicks your butt, it's not impossible because the hard work done in advance makes those last few miles achievable.

FROM ARMOR BEARER TO ARMOR WEARER

In 1 Samuel 16, a kid named David was brought in from tending sheep and anointed as the future king of Israel. Oddly, he was then sent back out to the pasture. It wasn't until a while later that King Saul summoned David to the palace and made him his armor bearer.

David instantly went from shepherding to tending the king's heavy armor. The verses go on to say that when Saul was angry or upset, David would play music to calm him down.

When we recognize that there were quite a few opportunities for stewardship between David the shepherd and David the king, suddenly his final role makes a lot more sense. The jump from field hand to king is a picture of wild obedience and a pretty crazy story. But when we take into account pieces of the puzzle along the way, we see how the hard work prepared him for the end.

I looked into what it meant to be an armor bearer and learned some interesting things. To bear the arms of a warrior was a servant's role. It was a role that meant he was with the king in war, close enough to dress the king for battle, listen to strategy and politics, watch how he commanded his men, and take the bloodied gear off at the end of battle. Before the Lord asked David to lead men into battle, He allowed him to see it firsthand. God even allowed David to see the humanity of the man beneath the armor and calm his spirit with music.

By learning to tend sheep first, David learned how to serve. When his service moved from sheep to people, he knew how to humble himself. In bearing armor for a king, he saw and experienced things that would prepare him for the next step. David learned to steward well, and each responsibility along the way eventually prepared him to be a king.

God clearly anointed David for great things, but before David walked into those things, he walked a series of smaller obedient steps along the way. Before any of his obedience seemed wild to anyone else, it was faithful and diligent before the Lord.

We serve a good God who equips us in steps of obedience along the way for the tasks He calls us to do.

Do you feel that the Lord has anointed you and called you, like David, to something specific? If so, walk obediently toward the thing you feel God's calling you to and steward your steps for the end goal.

PINTEREST-PERFECT PEOPLE

I've noticed that a large number of people feel the Lord has given them a clear picture of what they're being called into for His kingdom. It's beautiful to have the opportunity of seeing so many people to whom the Lord has given a specific calling. But what I also see is a whole lot of exhausted striving. A whole lot of people trying superhard, analyzing this and that, trying to make the most out of every opportunity and never miss out. Because if we miss out on this, then we won't be able to meet the people we need to meet to do the huge things that the Lord wants us to do next. Right?

It's as if we think we have to keep up with the Joneses. And at times, keeping up isn't about envy as much as it is about fear. It's easy to think that we could miss out on things. And sometimes we will miss out on fun things, good things, enjoyable things … and friends. *That's okay.* If we're stewarding this life, then we want to be a people who aren't just living but are living well … living full … living wisely. Let me share a few verses with you from Proverbs:

> My son, if you receive my words
> > and treasure up my commandments with
> > > you,
> making your ear attentive to wisdom
> > and inclining your heart to
> > > understanding;
> yes, if you call out for insight
> > and raise your voice for understanding,

> if you seek it like silver
>> and search for it as for hidden treasures,
> then you will understand the fear of the LORD
>> and find the knowledge of God.
> For the LORD gives wisdom;
>> from his mouth come knowledge and
>> understanding;
> he stores up sound wisdom for the upright;
>> he is a shield to those who walk in
>> integrity,
> guarding the paths of justice
>> and watching over the way of his saints.
> Then you will understand righteousness and
>> justice
>> and equity, every good path;
> for wisdom will come into your heart,
>> and knowledge will be pleasant to your soul;
> discretion will watch over you,
>> understanding will guard you. (2:1–11)

If we receive God's words and treasure His commands, then we'll walk in wisdom, knowledge, discretion, and understanding.

Pastor Charles Stanley has been quoted as saying, "If you tell God no because He won't explain the reason He wants you to do something, you are actually hindering His blessing. But when you say yes to Him, all of heaven opens to pour out His goodness and reward your obedience. What matters more than material blessings are the things He is teaching us in our spirit."

When the Israelites walked in obedience to God, their lives overflowed with His blessings. God promised the people,

> If you faithfully obey the voice of the LORD your God, being careful to do all his commandments that I command you today, the LORD your God will set you high above all the nations of the earth. And all these blessings shall come upon you and overtake you, if you obey the voice of the LORD your God. Blessed shall you be in the city, and blessed shall you be in the field. Blessed shall be the fruit of your womb and the fruit of your ground and the fruit of your cattle, the increase of your herds and the young of your flock. Blessed shall be your basket and your kneading bowl. Blessed shall you be when you come in, and blessed shall you be when you go out. (Deut. 28:1–6)

After all those great benefits of obedience, Deuteronomy pretty much lays the smackdown for disobedience. It's been said, "The ship that will not obey the helm will have to obey the rocks."

What does this mean for us today? The modern social-media world we live in is fast paced. Five minutes on Facebook, Twitter, or Pinterest, and you'll suddenly feel like you're not doing enough. Your blog following isn't big enough, or your dinners aren't beautiful enough. Your kids' crafts aren't crafty enough, or your house isn't magazine worthy. It can be a defeating space that makes you think you aren't enough. Your screens and feeds yell out that if you aren't doing these things, you're squandering your gifts or opportunities. Worse, maybe you never had gifts and opportunities to begin with.

But that is a lie.

We may think we have to meet Pinterest perfection to matter in the world or for the Lord to accomplish His purposes through us. But maybe, just maybe, the expectations we have and the "callings" we're following are an on-ramp to dissatisfaction with ourselves, our lives, or even our relationships with the Lord.

Maybe we think being obedient looks like a whole lot of work.

Ecclesiastes 4:6 says, "Better is a handful of quietness than two hands full of toil and a striving after wind." Isaiah 45 repeats the sentiment and reminds us where we are in the pecking order of the heavens:

> Woe to him who strives with him who formed
> him,
> a pot among earthen pots!
> Does the clay say to him who forms it, "What
> are you making?"
> or "Your work has no handles"? ...
>
> I made the earth
> and created man on it;
> it was my hands that stretched out the heavens,
> and I commanded all their host. (vv. 9, 12)

When we know the character of our good God, walking in His words and treasuring His commands, we receive wisdom, understanding, and blessing. If we're following the Lord and being obedient to the things He is asking us individually to do, we won't *ever* actually miss out on anything good that He has for us.

Did you get that? When we walk in obedience to the Lord, we won't ever actually miss out on anything that He has for us. When we start thinking about obedience in that way, it not only begins to *not* feel wild or even hard, but also becomes necessary for full living ... for free living.

At the Allume conference last year, an attendee came up and thanked me for the work put into such a large event. She asked, "How are you so brave?"

I clearly remember being shocked at the question and saying, "Brave, nothing. I'm just wanting to be obedient."

The thing I've been learning about obedience is that it has everything to do with following. Obedience doesn't mean just setting goals and doing what we have to do to reach them. It's about curiosity, faithful listening, and following through. It's about a lot of yeses to the small things and the hard things. Obedience is about diligence to pursue God's heart, not our purposes. It has everything to do with following and nothing to do with striving.

CURIOUS CORNERS

God ordered the stars. He fed five thousand people with just a little bit of food. In the economy of God, He likes to take very little and make much.

My tiny yes to a dormitory dinner party became the first in a series of yeses that led to my hosting 450 women from all around the continent at Allume. To some on the outside, saying yes to Allume may have looked like an act of wild obedience. It seemed to everyone, including me, to come out of nowhere. But, really, when I think about it, it was just simply the next "okay."

For me, saying yes to the Lord came after saying yes to dorm dinner parties, yes to selling radio advertising, yes to running my own jewelry-making business, and so on. It came after yeses to invite people into my home and my heart, and nos to working other places. It came after tiny yeses to discipling small groups of women in my home, and yes to leading, learning, teaching, and submitting over many years. Like King David, we spend a whole lot of years as shepherds and armor bearers and never even know sometimes where any of it is going.

Walking by faith and not by sight means never actually worrying where we're going. Being obedient can also feel like the place full of more possibility than we can even imagine. Sometimes being wildly obedient really just means being consistently obedient. Being more worried about the diligence of obedience than the place where we think we could be headed. It's walking curiously around little corners instead of through wide gates and discovering the fullness within small steps that teach us how to sometimes jump toward greater ones.

Wild obedience is tending sheep in obscurity. It's bearing armor for a king as a contented servant. It's witnessing battles and moving into new territories. Wild obedience begins with saying yes to loving people and eventually maybe even moves to rescuing some from dark-alley brothels in Southeast Asia. It's inviting people into our lives and sharing community around tattered tables and imperfect egg custards. Really, wild obedience isn't that wild; it's just learning to wisely steward the gifts and moments of life the Lord gives us along the way.

Chapter 12

Continual Soul Work

*Oh my Lord and my God! How stupendous is Thy grandeur!
We are like so many foolish peasant lads: we think we know
something of Thee, yet it must be comparatively nothing, for there
are profound secrets even in ourselves of which we know naught.*

Teresa of Avila

I didn't fit in at all. I walked with our group through the market with low-hanging ceilings and concrete pillars supporting the crumbling structure. I stared at floors drenched in the blood of freshly butchered animals. Men shouted at me in a language I didn't understand. I stuck out like a sore thumb. It didn't matter that I had on the traditional *salwar kameez* dress and wrap, modest-looking shoes, and very little makeup. My skin was pasty white in comparison to their warm cappuccino complexions. I practically reflected the small bits of light sneaking in through gaps in the fabric-tapestry roof above us.

I felt so out of place. *They shouldn't be yelling at us like this. They mean to disrespect us,* I thought. I'd read the book on the cultural differences and knew that men speaking to women they didn't know was taboo. Certainly waving frantically in our faces and reaching out to touch us as we walked past was far outside the bounds of cultural appropriateness. I couldn't wait to exit the market. The smell of fish and fruit and feces was pungent in the air. My nostrils felt singed from the open gas flames cooking meat around me. My heart raced faster, and I just wanted to leave.

Finally outside the market, we began to walk along the dirty river running through Dhaka, Bangladesh. Tiny stick and metal structures scattered along the edge of the river were home to the children running pantless alongside us. It looked nothing like my home. We were novelty items moving through foreign streets. The children reached for us with dirty and malnourished hands, asked questions in indiscernible Bangla, and rubbed infection from their tiny noses. We passed men missing limbs, crumpled along the walls separating the river from partially built apartments above. I looked up at the homes without walls, nothing more than a stack of open concrete levels soaring into the air, and prayed that the people living seven stories up wouldn't fall and die before my eyes. Even earnest prayers that the thin sheets-for-walls could somehow contain the children whose voices I heard echoing back down to the street gave me very little confidence that my fears wouldn't come true.

I felt my chest tighten and a knot form in my throat. My eyes began to water, and words gathered in my throbbing skull, hidden deep behind bone and flesh, reticent to be spoken into the air.

God, what is up with this? I thought. *Why did You bring me here? I'm afraid I'm just going to offend people. My big southern smile and touchy-feely personality are a complete abomination to this entire culture.*

Where composure and restraint are valued, I'm gregarious and outgoing. I'm no good in this place. Why am I here? I want to go home ... I just want to leave. I hate it here. Everything about my personality seemed to conflict with the traits this culture valued in women.

I walked along in silence, every muscle in my chest and face choking back the tears I was afraid would come and not stop. I'd traveled halfway around the world to get here. I was on a writing trip with an organization called Food for the Hungry to see its work in and around Dhaka, the capital of Bangladesh and the ninth most populated city in the world. When my friend Lindsey had asked me to come just a couple of months earlier, I thought, *If I don't do this, there's pretty much no chance I'll ever actually go to Bangladesh on purpose.*

I had to look the country up on my children's globe. I was pretty sure that it was near India, but I couldn't put my finger on it exactly. The most I knew about Bangladesh was that its name showed up on dozens of tags stitched to the clothes hanging in my closet. It was a third-world country and among the most densely populated on the earth. I knew so very little but was curious about what God could have for me there.

I'm an idiot. I never should have come, I scolded myself harshly.

"Are you okay?" My friend Daniel sidled up to me as we turned onto a busy street and exited the river walk.

My lips could barely form the word *no* before the tears began. I felt ashamed. Here was the opportunity of a lifetime, and I was falling apart. Losing my composure, I pinched my eyes and slapped my cheeks. I stepped in a pool of urine to avoid falling in a hole sunk deep in the sidewalk.

"What's going on?" he asked. "You're not saying a word. That's not you.... You're a verbal processor. What's in that head of yours?"

"I shouldn't be here," I said as I walked ahead of him to carve out some space by myself.

I went to sleep that night with earphones stuck in my ears to drown out the thoughts beckoning me to hop on the next plane back to America.

Waking up the next morning around four o'clock, I didn't feel much different from when I had fallen asleep. My entire body clock was a disaster with an eleven-hour time difference confusing my sleep patterns. In addition to my mixed-up emotions, I was even getting my nights and days confused. I felt like a jumbled mess of time and emotion.

I can't do this again, Lord, I silently prayed. Getting some rest had moved me away from the brink of tears, but I was still afraid to spend another day so outside of myself.

I don't know how to fit in here. I don't know how to be a version of myself that makes sense in this culture.

Cracking open my Bible, I began searching for any bit of hope that would tell me I'd be okay. I wanted some word to let me know that I wasn't a complete waste of an expensive plane ticket across the planet.

Just love. Those words rang in my mind. Simple, pure, uncomplicated. *Be you. Just love.*

What? But how do I do that, Lord? How do I love here when my version of love doesn't fit? I don't speak the language; they don't even understand me.

At that moment, the pages of my Bible fell open to a well-worn passage:

> If I speak in the tongues of men and of angels, but have not love, I am a noisy gong or a clanging cymbal. And if I have prophetic powers, and understand all mysteries and all knowledge, and if I have all faith, so as to remove mountains, but have not love, I am nothing. If I give away all I have, and if I deliver up my body to be burned, but have not love, I gain nothing.
>
> Love is patient and kind; love does not envy or boast; it is not arrogant or rude. It does not insist on its own way; it is not irritable or resentful; it does not rejoice at wrongdoing, but rejoices with the truth. Love bears all things, believes all things, hopes all things, endures all things. Love never ends. (1 Cor. 13:1–8)

Be you. Just love.

Suddenly I knew the answer. It didn't matter whether I could speak Bangla if I couldn't speak in love.

I was the only me, and God didn't bring me here to become an entirely different version of myself. He had no desire to chop up my personality and put me back together piecemeal so that I would fit in. If I denied the way God made me, then perhaps I wouldn't even be able to achieve the purposes He had for me here. Or anywhere, for that matter.

CONTINUE

In his timeless classic *Mere Christianity*, C. S. Lewis wrote,

> Your real, new self (which is Christ's and also yours, and yours just because it is His) will not come as long as you are looking for it. It will come when you are looking for Him. Does that sound strange? The same principle holds, you know, for more everyday matters. Even in social life, you will never make a good impression on other people until you stop thinking about what sort of impression you are making. Even in literature and art, no man who bothers about originality will ever be original; whereas if you simply try to tell the truth (without caring twopence how often it has been told before) you will, nine times out of ten, become original without ever having noticed it. The principle runs through all life from top to bottom. Give up yourself, and you will find your real self. Lose your life and you will save it. Submit to death, death of your ambitions and favourite wishes every day and death of your whole body in the end; submit with every fibre of your being, and you will find eternal life. Keep back nothing. Nothing that you have not given away will be really yours. Nothing in you that has not died will ever be raised from the dead. Look for yourself, and you will find in the long run only

hatred, loneliness, despair, rage, ruin, and decay. But look for Christ and you will find Him, and with Him everything else thrown in.[1]

We all long to fit in, whether we're in a small group of friends or an entirely different culture. Inadvertently soliciting the stares and judgments of strangers makes us feel uncomfortable. We want to be accepted, and when we think we won't be, we bend over backward for approval. We are fearfully, wonderfully, and uniquely made. If God had wanted two of the exact same person, He'd have made them. By dismissing the unique gifts, bents, tendencies, and personalities we have, we actually rob God's kingdom of what only we can individually do. Even when we think we don't make sense, or life doesn't make sense, we have to keep moving. We have to keep living.

In John 17, Jesus prayed in the garden before He was taken into custody. There amid His cry for deliverance from certain death, we find the word *continue*. Tucked beside God's love for us is a call to carry on, to move forward, to pursue the roles we're given to fulfill in making Him known to the world. Even in His final moments, Jesus breathed,

> O righteous Father, even though the world does not know you, I know you, and these know that you have sent me. I made known to them your name, and I will continue to make it known, that the love with which you have loved me may be in them, and I in them. (vv. 25–26)

Continue means "to persist, to resume after interruption, to move forward." I love that, don't you? Continuing is to resume after interruption. Make no mistake. In case you haven't already figured it out, the reality is that whatever happens in your life, in your plan, it'll get interrupted sooner or later. In fact, I think most of life is one giant interruption if we think of it in terms of our own master plans. But we can't allow the things that interrupt us to stop or cripple us in our walk toward Jesus.

The apostle Paul said it this way:

> Brothers, I do not consider that I have made it my own. But one thing I do: forgetting what lies behind and straining forward to what lies ahead, I press on toward the goal for the prize of the upward call of God in Christ Jesus. (Phil. 3:13–14)

If we want to continue in our faith and walk in curiosity after the things God has for us but has yet to reveal, we have to get back up when we fall down. We have to try again. We have to know that when God says His mercies are new every morning (see Lam. 3:22–23), He means it. No matter how heavy the past looks, if we want to keep moving forward, we can't spend all our time grasping at the straws of the past. We must resume after interruption.

One day, with laundry piled high on the bed, I snapped a photo of that reality towering high before me and shared it on Instagram. An old friend from high school replied and said something about Sisyphus. I had no idea who Sisyphus was and had to google it. Turns out, Sisyphus was a king from Greek mythology known for his deceitfulness and iron-fisted rule. He apparently thought he could outthink the god Zeus, and somewhere along the way, he betrayed a confidence they had. In turn, Zeus cursed Sisyphus to eternally rolling a rock up a hill.

That stinks …

Sometimes I think we all feel a little bit like Sisyphus. Laundry feels like a Sisyphean task, for sure. But don't you feel sometimes as if you're forever rolling a boulder uphill too? We see areas of our lives that need work, and instead of looking at them like new days dawning, we allow ourselves to feel as though we're on the downhill side of an uphill boulder roll. Life begins to feel crushing. Never mind moving forward; we're doing good not to have everything we're pushing roll back over the top of us and break us.

What in your past could be holding you back? What obstacle is keeping you from moving forward? What fears, issues, or broken pieces of your life do you think disqualify you from moving forward? What habit do you need to break? What sin is enslaving you that makes you feel beyond repair? What parts of your personality do you feel hinder your forward movement? Our work is never done, but that, my friend, is less of a Sisyphean task than it is an opportunity for new dawnings.

Even if it looks different from what you thought, don't minimize your contribution to the kingdom. The beauty of transforming our minds is that we don't have to conform to the patterns the world tells us we should fit into. In constantly submitting ourselves to the work of the cross, allowing the Lord to work in and through us, we can recognize that we are individually gifted to make unique stamps on the world.

Take what is behind you and make it new. Just because you may not think you're the version of yourself that you're meant to be doesn't mean that God thinks the same. He wants to know that you'll keep seeking, curiously pursuing His opportunities for you, pushing forward, and, in doing so, finding more of yourself through Him. He wants to know that even when you can't make sense of what you're doing, you'll continue to follow after Him. A life lived in process involves a continuous and curious pursuit.

CULTIVATE CURIOSITY

I love my life. I'm blessed with a happy marriage and children I adore (and who, in all fairness, make me nuts sometimes too). I've had the privilege of leading a ministry for several years and spent some time homeschooling our kids. It's a really great life, and I'm beyond grateful for it. But I began to realize that in fulfilling so many of my duties, I was losing my curiosity. I felt myself slipping into the monotony of repeated patterns, and my soul felt as if it was starving.

Continuous curiosity requires work, and I'm learning that I need to make different kinds of space along the way. Sometimes I find myself desperate for something that feels as if it wakes up my senses again, and so I consider drastic measures.

In *Secrets of the Secret Place*, Bob Sorge said that one of the keys to increasing our spiritual grounding is to create space. He suggests literally shutting the door to our rooms, going on a retreat alone for a few days, and intentionally making enough dead space so that we can't help but spend time deep in the Word with the Lord.

Friend, I know that's a *hard* thing to do. Even when I wake early, tiptoe out of my room, and slip away by myself, I swear that my kids can sense the vibrations of movement in the house. Minutes after I find some quiet space, it's interrupted. And when my kids aren't interrupting the space I've carved out, my own mind wanders. *What's for dinner? Don't forget to switch the laundry. Call the HVAC guy to fix the air-conditioning. Today is Tonia's birthday; call her.* The list in my brain is as distracting as the little people bounding into my room.

Despite the distractions, we have to keep making space. Keep going in a room alone and shutting the door. Keep a pen and paper beside you just to write down the list of things you don't want to forget. Making space requires practical measures to clear the air as much as possible. Some days we may not hear anything from God. But we keep getting up, keep shutting a door during a quiet moment, and keep seeking so that we can hear. We make little spaces along the way to create breathing room, and those little bits of space can keep us sustained along the way.

I'll be honest. I've ended up needing to employ drastic measures to create space to hear God because of my own inability recently to make the little pockets of space I need. Do you think that admission disqualifies me from telling you to make the space? Can we be honest, though, and acknowledge that it happens to all of us? We get into ruts, and we forget how to get out. Sometimes we have to do something drastic to snap ourselves out of our patterns.

I've watched some women choose drastic measures that take them away from marriages and families, never to return. I get that life can feel crushing, and we all want to escape pieces of it from time to time. But there has to be a better way to find refreshment in the journey before it cripples us from functioning in our normal roles.

When I began to feel suffocated writing this book, I took drastic measures and spontaneously booked a ticket to visit friends in Oxford, England, for a few soul-filling days. While there, I made space to go to the Sheldonian Theatre to hear a cellist play the Bach cello suites. We saw a sign advertising the concert as we were walking by the theater and spontaneously decided to check it out. It cost the equivalent of about fourteen dollars to soak up the sounds that echoed around the room for ninety minutes. As the music bounced from painted ceiling to wooden floors, reverberating off the leaded-glass windows all around us, I felt my spirit sway peacefully along with the melody.

The trip to England was pulled together just two weeks before I arrived. The spontaneous decision itself felt invigorating. Please know I realize that it's entirely impractical to go gallivanting around the globe just to feed our dwindling curiosity. Honestly, if it weren't for my parents, who were already going to be watching my children; a supersupportive husband who helped pave the way; and friends who let me stay with them for free, I wouldn't have done it. It seemed that the stars aligned in my favor. In fact, since I married, I'd never done anything like this by myself. It's perhaps the craziest thing I've ever done. Ever.

Friends began messaging me from all over the country …

"That's so cool that you just decided to do something and are doing it …"

"I wish I could be spontaneous to do something for myself that's life giving too …"

"I need a break so badly. Will you pack me in your suitcase?"

Over and over I heard the same thing ... desperation. We're killing ourselves by forgetting to do things that are life giving to our own souls. How do we recover these life-giving moments? My buddy John makes big, fancy knives in his free time. My friend Katie breaks out her set of five-dollar watercolors and paints late into the night. There are little things we each love to do, but so often we don't make the space to do them.

I met someone once who knew a lot of fascinating research about the human brain. Apparently there are pathways in our brains that information travels along. Over time, especially as we get older, some of those pathways become well worn and well traveled as we lean into making the same kinds of decisions over and over. Eventually it's almost as though our brains forget how to travel outside those pathways, so we fall into routines that can begin to make us feel bored. I think most of the time we don't even realize that we're actually boring ourselves. Really, we allow ourselves to make the same decisions over and over, and thus we forget how to do new and exciting things. We can train ourselves right out of living curious.

Every time I go to McAlister's Deli, I order the same thing: half of a southwestern cobb salad and half of a grilled-chicken spud with jalapeños. I really like it. Usually I eat half for dinner and the other half for lunch the next day. I think I've ordered the same thing for probably five years. I'm a little bit afraid that I won't like something different, so I just keep getting the same thing.

The one time I did break the mold and ordered something different, I didn't like it as much. I was disappointed. So to avoid further disappointment, I just keep sticking with what I know works for me.

After moving to a new house, my husband and I realized that there were several new restaurants nearby that we hadn't tried before. My five-year-old announced one day, "We should try lots of new places that are near us now."

So we have. There's a McAlister's Deli nearby, something I know I like, but the more new places we've tried, the less I find myself wanting to return to the old standbys.

It takes a bit more effort to try new places and new things. I have to pay closer attention as I'm driving to notice what is along the way. I have to think a little bit harder than sitting at home, recalling what all I've seen that are viable options. I can't be so lazy. I definitely risk disappointment when I go somewhere new, but so far that has happened significantly less than I might have thought. Our family has had a ton of fun in the discovery. For instance, we found a spot that makes funnel cakes.

"It's like an edible angel," my oldest son said.

"This is so fun, Mommy!" exclaimed my youngest.

Now we have powdered-sugar-coated memories that came from moving outside our comfort zones.

Friend, even when you and I remember to do things that feel fulfilling, we can forget to engage in experiences that breed further curiosity, like wandering down an unfamiliar street, ordering something different on the menu from a favorite takeout, or driving home a different way. Sometimes we just need to break out of our patterns. We need to remember that God is good and the risk of exploration is really offering us the opportunity for adventure.

I wondered why I needed to go to Oxford to remember that there is so much goodness all around me. For all the beauty surrounding me in the Sheldonian Theatre, I closed my eyes as I swayed and felt the music play. It didn't really matter where I was in that moment. Even when I can see beauty, sometimes I just need to remember how to feel it. I have to remember what it is to feel alive if I want to pursue life and God curiously.

Before I left for England, I got up early on Saturday morning, put on my tennis shoes, and went for a walk around my neighborhood in the crisp spring air. By the time I got home, my mind felt refreshed and my skin glistened with beads of sweat releasing retained bits of the previous day. I felt alive.

As unexciting as it sounds, we have to be intentional to create space for self-care and time alone with God. Maybe it's giving your spouse a day off for a hike in the mountains with a backpack and a Bible. Maybe it's making space on a weekend morning for reading the book you've cracked open every night for the past twelve months, only to fall asleep midway through the first chapter each time. Relax into conversation on the porch with your spouse after the kids are in bed, no matter how exhausted you both feel. Explore parts of your town that you haven't seen before. Visit a new restaurant. Take a walk in an unfamiliar park. Risk being a little bit outside of yourself. I'm willing to bet that you'll even discover new parts of yourself along the way.

We feel alive when we give ourselves permission to really live, try new things, meet new people, and have conversations about different topics than usual. So make friends with someone you wouldn't normally befriend. Volunteer in your community. Intentionally rub shoulders with people who have had different experiences than you. Read a different kind of book. Walk through an art museum that's outside your normal preference, and look for the beauty outside your natural bent. If we allow the things we explore to become mundane, then perhaps we aren't opening ourselves to the creativity of God in the world around us. We may not see the world change immediately with our singular, small decisions, but they can certainly begin to change our individual lives.

Perhaps you have an idea that doesn't necessarily feel world changing. If you just tease it out a little bit, though, what if it could? If I did this, what might happen? Imagine if we did …? What if we just …?

TEASE IT OUT A LITTLE

My friend Jessica and her husband were in the process of adopting their son from Rwanda several years ago. International adoption costs a pretty penny, so she decided that on a trip to Africa to see their soon-to-be son, she would buy a few handmade goods to come home and sell to help raise money to fund their adoption. People went nuts over the jewelry and bags she brought back. So the next time she went, she began placing orders with the village women so she could return home with more goods to sell.

Everything started with a simple idea to be resourceful and help fund the adoption. But it has turned into an incredible grow-ing business called Noonday Collection, which sells jewelry made by artisans all over the world. The purchases help village men and women from around the globe support their families, as well as creating flexible job opportunities for women here in the States to be sales ambassadors. One idea that wasn't necessarily earth shattering, when teased out a bit, when curiously followed into a "Next, what if we …?" sort of mentality, has become a business that is affecting families all over the globe. Take a little thing you love and tease it out.

Ashley loves to paint. It's soul filling for her. So she signed up to take a few classes at a local community center. At church some needs arose for a small-group project serving a local ministry that helped abused children. First Ashley used her passion to help decorate the space to make it more friendly for the kids. Because it was a passion for her, it seemed an easy step to invest with something she already enjoyed. Later she was able to share that love with the children when she was asked to lead some craft projects with them at the home. Take a little thing you love and tease it out.

Katie has always had a passion for children in the foster-care system. Over the years she volunteered at a Department of Social Services office. She noticed a need for clothing as children entered the system and were placed in new home environments. When she was getting rid of some clothes that didn't fit her kids anymore, she donated them. As the need grew, she asked a few friends to donate some of their items as well. Doing what she could at first led her to eventually collect vanloads full of clothes from an entire church. Take a little thing you love and tease it out.

Think of something that piques your interest. Give it a shot. Do it. Take the next step, and then maybe the next. One tiny yes at a time, and you just never know where you might land. Grab an idea and kick it around a bit. Tease it out a little. Throw in a few other ideas. See what the Lord may do when you're willing to submit to Him and follow where He could take you. Maybe along the way, you'll see a few things change. Maybe you'll see yourself change. Even better, you might see your curiosity grow for more of God and what He could have for you.

LOSING IS FINDING

Wondering still what God could have for me in this place, I collected my thoughts and walked into the lobby of the Dhaka hotel to meet my team

"Hey, are you doing better today?" Daniel asked as he met me at the bottom of the steps.

"I think so. It's going to be okay."

We loaded up the van and made our way through concrete slums piled high on either side with burning trash and debris. Our van crept along, navigating the narrow streets filled with people and animals as we made our way back to the iron gates of a small school tucked deep in the middle of this impoverished neighborhood. Children saw our pale faces peering out of the van windows and began to run alongside, banging on the windows, waving, and smiling.

Be you. Just love. Keep moving. One foot in front of the other.

The van came to a stop, and the door slid open. A few dozen children began reaching for us, shouting and smiling. I didn't know what they were saying. Before I was even all the way out of the van, a tiny girl, dirty faced, with twinkling eyes and bright white teeth, grabbed my hand. I stooped low and pulled her close. I smiled my widest, toothiest grin and said "Hi" as I hugged her. As soon as the child next to her saw what I'd done, she was shoving the first girl aside and grabbing my neck, which was still bent forward from the first encounter. "Hi," I said, hugging tightly this new child with a set of sparkling eyes. She squeezed me right back, a smile spread wide across her face.

Once the other children noticed what was happening, I could barely walk forward for all the arms reaching out to grab hold of me. A swarm of thin hands grabbed at my clothes, small voices desperate for the affection that I was tossing out like free candy at a parade.

"Hi! Hi! Hi! Hi! Hi! Hi!" Their tiny voices laughed and repeated my own cheerful greeting back to me. As I was surrounded by all these new faces, the muscles in my jaw began to feel sore. My own smile pulled tight across my face, and I knew this was just where I was supposed to be. Just me. Moving forward just as I am. Just loving.

When we make space to step outside of ourselves, it can take a bit to catch up with knowing who we're meant to be. Sometimes we must lose ourselves to find ourselves. But I've found that when I lose myself, I find God. Interestingly enough, in looking for more of God, you'll be surprised how much of yourself you'll discover without even trying.

Chapter 13

Pursuing a Curious Faith

*The real voyage of discovery consists not in seeking
new landscapes, but in having new eyes.*

Marcel Proust

In 1960 the Roanoke and Blackwater Rivers in the mountains of
Virginia were dammed up at the Smith Mountain gorge to harness
power and generate electricity. It took three years for the dam to
be completed. My grandfather bought a whole bunch of random
land on top of some pretty high hills in Huddleston, Virginia, in
1964 because he anticipated the value of what was to come. By 1966,
Smith Mountain Lake was completely formed, and my granddad
owned practically an entire point of valuable lakefront property. He
knew that what was coming was worth the early investment and
made choices to live in a way that anticipated future benefits.

Curiosity anticipates hope. It moves forward toward what we
believe will come. It invests in places that may or may not yield the
results we want, in the belief that our future is hopeful.

I'm sitting on that lakefront property this minute. My children now enjoy fishing off the dock, kayaking around the bends of the land, and swimming in the cool mountain waters. Granddad bought the land, crossed his fingers, and hoped the property wouldn't end up underwater. He was pretty sure it would still be there once the lake was full, but there was a chance it wouldn't. He bought it anyway. Curiosity takes chances. And as I sit with a cup of coffee on a porch, overlooking a vast lake of shining waters, I find myself overwhelmingly grateful for the legacy of curiosity that has been left to me.

Funny thing about a legacy: you can't leave one that you're unwilling to invest in first yourself. If we want to inhabit lands of promise to pass on to future generations, we have to be willing to walk into them while we have the chance.

There's nothing I hope for more than to see my children grow up and love Jesus. To become men of God who love His people and serve this world with integrity and compassion. On my knees I ask the Lord to make my sons strong and humble men who will fight for justice and care for the poor and broken. Of course I want them to experience success in life, but the way I define that has changed over the years.

I find myself realizing that the success I want them to experience, whether it's in corporate America or at the ends of the earth, is the knowledge that God is good and that He is for them. That whatever they do, wherever they go, they'll walk in the freedom and curiosity that are found when they trust God and follow Him.

I want to leave a legacy of faith that gets passed from generation to generation. I want my children's children to remember the way we lived and take those nuggets to do even greater things themselves. I want to walk into the lands intended for me so that my children will live in the fullness of those promises too. I want to overcome giants myself to inhabit places ripe with fruit so that I can teach my children how to do the same. "I believe that I shall look upon the goodness of the LORD in the land of the living!" (Ps. 27:13), and I want my children to know that that goodness is for them too. I hope that the same grace and mercy, the same blood of redemption that marks my life, will mark theirs as well.

I want to live like Caleb and Joshua, trusting that what the Lord says, He means. That the promises of heaven are for me because He says they are. Sure, there are giants in the land, but He says,

> In all these things we are more than conquerors through him who loved us. For I am sure that neither death nor life, nor angels nor rulers, nor things present nor things to come, nor powers, nor height nor depth, nor anything else in all creation, will be able to separate us from the love of God in Christ Jesus our Lord. (Rom. 8:37–39)

If we want to inhabit the lands of promise in our lives and leave a legacy of hope, we must first root ourselves in the goodness of God. We must see His power and experience His might and move forward to pursue Him. He is the God who covers moons. He is the God who defeats giants in our behalf. The Lord is with us. The Lord is with you. His goodness precedes your journey and inhabits your going and coming. Don't forget that.

When the people of Israel refused to believe Caleb and Joshua's words, when they feared that the giants in the land would overcome them, Caleb and Joshua tore their clothing and wept aloud, pleading with the people,

> "The land, which we passed through to spy it out, is an exceedingly good land. If the LORD delights in us, he will bring us into this land and give it to us, a land that flows with milk and honey. Only do not rebel against the LORD. And do not fear the people of the land, for they are bread for us. Their protection is removed from them, and the LORD is with us; do not fear them." Then all the congregation said to stone them with stones. But the glory of the LORD appeared at the tent of meeting to all the people of Israel. (Num. 14:7–10)

God calls us His beloved and knows not only the number of hairs on our heads but also the depths of the longings in our souls. The truth of our broken lives is found in the resurrection of His, and when we release control and settle into trust, when we tune our ears to hear the sound of His voice, freedom and joy can be found all around us. The end of ourselves is the beginning of Him, and the wandering and waiting that once made us feel lost can now prepare us for more. Fear, worry, and tension wash away as we're no longer defined by our circumstances but instead are aligned vertically with the purposes of heaven. We'll never miss out on the goodness of God in our lives. No matter how we mess up or struggle along the way, there is no place we can go where He won't be. No matter how tangled we feel in the tensions, no matter the depth of heavy things we carry, the rooting and redemption of Christ will be enough to bring us back to life.

MEME

Meme was tall and thin, with white hair piled like a puffy cloud on top of her head. She wore perfectly creased nylon slacks with flowery pastel blouses and always sat at an old phone table in the hallway outside her bedroom to take calls. Every time we went to Florida to visit my mom's side of the family, she invited my sister and me to the Golden Corral to eat our fill of macaroni and cheese and strawberry-banana Jell-O goo before we went back to her house for a spend-the-night party. Meme was fascinating to us.

In her eighties, as I knew her, she had lived what I thought was pretty much the coolest life ever. She kept a Sonitrol remote control in the bathroom and one by her bed to call for emergency assistance in case she fell, but the last thing this woman ever seemed to me to be was brittle or unable to get back up.

The tile floor in her Florida living room was covered with a zebra skin she got from a safari in Africa. A gazelle head was mounted on the wall at the back of the room over the wicker sofa. Ancient elephant tusks crisscrossed beneath the gazelle, and an otter skin draped over the end of the guest-room bed. My parents still have the bighorn sheep that her husband, Pappy, shot some eternity ago in the Yukon, and the bear head over the bed in my aunt's guest room always terrified me when we went to visit. Meme liked to divvy up the goods. The evidence of her life was spread in bits and pieces among the whole family.

My sister, Peyton, and I used to curl up on a pile of sofa cushions in the middle of the zebra rug as Meme showed us old slides and silent home videos of the adventures she and Pappy had taken. Pappy was a big-game hunter, and a longing for adventure ran hot in their veins. Mom told me that she remembers as a child seeing Meme and Pappy pull into their Lakeland, Florida, driveway with a moose head on top of a Buick station wagon. In the 1950s they drove the car all the way from Florida to the Alaska-Canadian Highway (which was dirt in many places) and into the Yukon Territory, where Meme stayed for weeks in a camp while Pappy hunted elk, caribou, moose, and bighorn sheep in the wilds.

Pappy was a car dealer by trade and swapped a new Buick every year to a Florida Everglades landowner for hunting access on sixty thousand acres, where Pappy parked a camper for weeks out of the year.

When Pappy died in the 1960s, Meme kept up her traveling ways. With friends and family, and even by herself when she couldn't find a companion, she traveled all over the world, collecting dolls. She rode the famous ocean liner the *Queen Elizabeth* to Europe, and on a trip to Scandinavia, she brought back little wooden shoes that we played with as children. The cuckoo clock and lederhosen from one trip to Germany were in my grandmother's guest room for years. I remember seeing slides of her perched high on a camel in sandy Morocco. On a visit to the Jordan River, she brought back water that my parents apparently used to christen me as a baby. My mother still displays an entire cabinet of dolls from Meme's travels to China, Yugoslavia, Japan, the Netherlands, Morocco and other African countries, Germany,

Scotland, England, and more. In a time when travel wasn't as simple as a quick and inexpensive plane ride, Meme overcame crazy obstacles to fully experience the world around her.

Certainly a life well lived isn't defined by the places we visit. But what Meme instilled in me as a child was a curiosity to experience the goodness of God's creation. And it's fair to say that I got bitten by the travel bug too, thanks to her. Married to an alcoholic, Meme wasn't without serious difficulties in her life, but she was a woman who didn't allow the hard things she experienced to steal her zeal for living. I remember her laughing, full of hope and possibility, even up until she died when I was around ten years old.

I learned from Meme that there's a whole lot of life we can experience and a whole lot of hardship we can push through when we cultivate a curiosity for what could come. She left a legacy of curiosity, and as the Lord has cultivated that in my life and revealed His goodness to me time and again, I find myself curiously pursuing hope with new abandon.

Catherine of Siena once said, "Be who God meant you to be and you will set the world on fire." I like to think she meant that rooting our faith in Him opens us to live with greater possibility, more passion, more fullness, and more hope for today and tomorrow. The goodness of God paves the way for us to steward our lives well.

In *Secrets of the Secret Place*, Bob Sorge said,

> Those who make decisions based upon external data become thermometers of society: Their lives reflect the natural forces that shape their destiny. But those who make their decisions based upon what they

see in God become thermostats of society: They influence their world through the forcefulness of bringing divinely received initiatives to bear upon this earthly sphere.[1]

We aren't promised a life without difficulty and struggle. In fact, we know there will be varying seasons that juxtapose each other, so it matters that we learn how to diligently and steadily navigate the swings. Understanding the goodness of God defines who we are and turns wilderness into a period of learning, worry into trust, waiting into joy, and hardship into redemption. Exchanging expectations we once held dear for a curious pursuit of God's goodness will open doors for fresh blessing. Rather than allowing outside circumstances to rob us of hope, when we pursue God, in His goodness, He transforms our entire perspective and uncovers the benefits of heaven all around us.

God's goodness is a vast river of promise, but if we want to experience it, at some point we have to decide to believe it for ourselves and jump in. Challenges, hardship, and struggle will come, but the character of God offers hope, possibility, and redemption when we pursue Him. Be who you were created to be, and you will set the world on fire, my friend.

SERIOUSLY ... CROCODILES!

I leaned over the split-rail fence and marveled that I was looking out onto the Nile. The Nile River. Yes, the one that showed up in the dreams of pharaohs and filled nets of biblical fishermen. The same Nile that turned to blood when touched by Moses's staff to showcase the power of a sovereign God. I stared out at the waters that American doctors had mentioned to me were filthy. Yet still I couldn't help but feel curious about the wooden sign to my right that marked a path down to a rope swing knotted tightly around an outstretched tree branch that hung probably sixty feet above sparkling water.

Through the leaves I saw someone pull the rope backward and launch forward with a tiny figure attached. Then I heard a squeal and a splash. Suddenly all I could think about were crocodiles.

The tree branches obstructing a clearer view began to agitate me, and before I knew it, my feet were kicking along the gravel road as I moved toward the sign marking the pathway to the water.

I watched three of my friends climb the rope and jump into the river, grabbing handfuls of mud as they pulled themselves back onto the slippery, red bank. My heart began to thunder inside my chest as I moved closer to the edge. This was the Nile River. I remembered again the fishermen's nets, Moses's staff, and the dreams of pharaohs. The Nile River. I was nearing the edge of the past … here in a present moment. What could this future of mine hold? What was to become of me?

I descended between the trees, grasping dirt and limbs as the ground beneath me gave way on the steep path to the bottom. I grabbed the long stretch of dangling rope and launched myself over the dirty, glistening water. A squeal, a splash, and then a decidedly nervous swim back to the slippery bank of the murky legend. With my feet kicking wildly, the frantic effort propelled me back up onto the sticky, red earth.

My heart thundered more, and I clambered back up the rocks to stand on the sturdy launching-pad root of a great old tree. I felt a smile creep into my soul that soon made its way across my face.

A million miles a minute, my mind raced with visions of Steve Irwin and a bunch of crocodiles. Then it slowed as I remembered Moses and the pharaohs, my life intersecting with theirs in this moment of history. The gentle waves lapped against the shore as I leaped off the root and careened into the water again. And again. Stories colliding. History with the present, fear with courage, curiosity with adventure, and the unknown with hope. The God of the Nile River was the same as the God of my present leaping ... the same God of my future pursuit.

The exploration of His goodness will rewrite our stories and breathe new life into us.

Believe me, I was afraid of crocodiles the entire time ... along with fish that could have sharp little teeth. I worried about giant lizards that most definitely have teeth, which I was certain circled underwater beneath my kicking feet. My mind raced, and I tried hard not to think long about what could be below me. I just plunged into the water and quickly made my way back to shore each time. I pretended to be brave and fearless as I jumped in over and over. But the truth is that I was scared the whole time ... because, seriously ... crocodiles!

Yet it was the Nile River, and I wanted to live the kind of life my kids and my kids' kids will want to tell stories about. I want to dip my toes into rivers of adventure and live swinging high on ropes of trust and curiosity, pursuing great faith and a great story with my great God. I want to overcome the things that keep me from moving forward, because I know that in His goodness, God gives me the capacity to do ... and to be.

I got a sinus infection the week after my grand leap into the river, so I picked up a preventive medicine from a Ugandan pharmacy before I left, just in case I'd been exposed to weird bacteria. Because sometimes ... the DANGER! But the fact remains that I swung on a rope and jumped into the Nile of history and of my right now.

Sometimes ... oftentimes ... really living can feel quite frankly a little bit unsafe, a little bit unsure. I keep finding that when I pursue God with a curious faith, I often end up with a brave one too.

But the Nile of Moses's era is the same Nile whose waters I swam. The God of Moses is the same for me too. The testimony of His goodness is a long one that I have resolved to fully trust. His promise is the same for me as it was for Joshua:

> Just as I was with Moses, so I will be with you. I will not leave you or forsake you. Be strong and courageous, for you shall cause this people to inherit the land that I swore to their fathers to give them. Only be strong and very courageous, being careful to do according to all the law that Moses my servant commanded you. Do not turn from it to the right hand or to the left, that you may have good success wherever you go. This Book of the Law shall not depart from your mouth, but you shall meditate on it day and night, so that you may be careful to do according to all that is written in it. For then you will make your way prosperous, and then you will have good success. Have I not commanded you? Be strong and courageous. Do not be frightened, and do not be dismayed, for the LORD your God is with you wherever you go. (Josh. 1:5–9)

We can't enjoy the fullness of adventure if we remain far away from engaging in the action … from engaging with God. Whoever said that real living was entirely safe anyhow?

C. S. Lewis, in his beloved series The Chronicles of Narnia, wrote,

> "Is [Aslan] a man?" asked Lucy.
>
> "Aslan a man!" said Mr. Beaver sternly. "Certainly not. I tell you he is the King of the wood and the son of the great Emperor-beyond-the-Sea. Don't you know who is the King of Beasts? Aslan is a lion—*the* Lion, the great Lion."
>
> "Ooh!" said Susan. "I'd thought he was a man. Is he—quite safe? I shall feel rather nervous about meeting a lion."
>
> "That you will, dearie, and no mistake," said Mrs. Beaver; "if there's anyone who can appear before Aslan without their knees knocking, they're either braver than most or else just silly."
>
> "Then he isn't safe?" said Lucy.
>
> "Safe?" said Mr. Beaver; "don't you hear what Mrs. Beaver tells you? Who said anything about being safe? 'Course he isn't safe. But he's good. He's the King, I tell you."[2]

A life on this earth will hold elements of danger, risk, and the unknown along the way. Pain, suffering, confusion, and missteps are all part of changing seasons. But as we explore our limitless God all around us, we open ourselves up to endless hope, joy, and possibility. A life lived hanging tight to the promise of Christ, curiously seeking more of Him—well, that's a legacy worth leaving. And a life worth living.

No matter the giants you face, you are destined to be victorious. Your faith in Christ has positioned you to be an overcomer … a strong and mighty warrior who takes lands and walks in promise. The life you live is shaped by your present capacity to believe the truth of God's goodness for you. Do you believe that He is good and that He is for you? Will you spend a lifetime in pursuit of the hope found only in Him? This is your present and your future. The certainty of our faith isn't found in where we're going but in the One we're following. This is living with curious faith.

Acknowledgments

To my God and my King. The more I come to know all three of You (Father, Son, and Holy Spirit), the more I stand in wonder. I can't keep from moving curiously to uncover a deeper relationship with You. It is never lost on me that in Your bigness You order the heavens, yet You still care about the state of my heart. You are never too busy, too distracted, or too overwhelmed to speak into my life, and Your goodness and mercy continue to make me want to live more curious than afraid. If I lost it all, I'd still have You. Every word of this is for You and because of You in my life.

To Jeremy. I couldn't do any of these things without your support and love. For all the ways you make me crazy, there are a million more ways you make me better. I married up … I'm sure of it. I'm so glad I get this whole life long to explore with you. I love you.

To Walker and Hudson. Your curiosity to uncover the world sparked my own. You lent me your eyes as my children, and through your lenses I see more of God in everything. It is my heart and my prayer that you pursue God with wild abandon and unquenchable curiosity for your whole lives. It will be hard, but you will never regret a life lived in passionate pursuit of the God who covers the moon. I love you both to that very moon and back.

Sarah Mae, my dearest heart friend, you have loved, supported, journeyed with, and encouraged me to do this. Your friendship is a gift I never even saw coming. Mimi and MaeMae forever.

Joanna, Lindsey, Lisa, Katie, Roxanne, and Karen, in celebration or heartbreak, I couldn't ask for friends more true. We have walked through life and death, through promise and brokenness together. Your friendships have been gifts to my spirit in ways only the heavenly Father could have known that I'd need. The words "thank you" don't encompass enough to even feel adequate. I love you, sisters so true.

Sara Hagerty, you are a kindred, and your encouragement and heart have been such a breath of fresh air to me in this season. Your friendship is life giving in so many ways.

Ann V., your friendship is balm. Thank you for your encouragement. One day we will sit on a porch for tea, and it will be magnificently unplanned and free. Annie Downs, thank you for reading this in bits and pieces and holding my hand along the way. I just adore you. And also you always make me laugh, which is medicine I'll take any day!

Mandy, you began as my assistant, but have become a lifelong friend. You deserve your own line for all the ways you keep me in line!

Carey, Christin, Amy, Tonya, Erin, Laura H., Jan, Mama D., and the rest of you who have invested along the way, Allume happens because of your love for the Lord, for me, and for the community of women it touches. I couldn't have done it any year without the investments that you made.

The Allume Community, who could have ever guessed that saying yes to this community could have blessed me with friendships and opportunities greater than I'd ever have dreamed for myself? You are a huge part of this walk of curious faith in my life. You are my people.

For my friends from Grace who shared a lot of my early adult years, I learned how to grieve hard things in my life with you first, and as a result I learned how to heal better too. Emily L., Kelley, Emily M., Taryn, Erica, Lindsey, and Miranda, your friendships have left lasting imprints on my life.

Don Jacobson, I never knew that signing with a literary agent would yield the kind of friendship that I've found with you. You have become a trusted mentor, spiritual father, and dear friend. You and Brenda feel like family to me, and I couldn't be more grateful that you have shepherded me through this process. I owe many thanks too to Lindsey Nobles, who made our initial acquaintance. Who'da thunk we'd have ended up here?

Blair Jacobson, you owe me a drink. If you hadn't pushed me with early edits the way you did and risked hurting my feelings to make me a better writer, there is no way I'd have emotionally withstood the grueling process of book writing and editing. On second thought, maybe I owe you one. Thank you!

Rob and Ashley Eagar of Wildfire Marketing, I'm not even sure where to begin. There are at least twenty thousand words on a cutting room floor somewhere thanks to your wisdom. These readers have no clue what you saved them from enduring beyond a litany of seventy-five-word sentences. They should thank you as much as I should, but let me say it for us all. Your publishing wisdom, literary support, and general encouragement have kept me sane when I thought I might be pushed to the edge. This has been so much fun with you guys along for the ride! I'll have wine and chocolate with you at four thirty any day, my friends!

Tim Peterson, you believed in me enough to convince the fine folks at David C Cook to print these pages. You took a chance on a new voice and I'll be forever grateful. Tim Close, Ingrid, Amy, Annette, Lisa B., Nicci H., Tiffany, and Chriscynethia, you guys are a rock-star team of people. I love the way Cook values relationship, and as a result I am so grateful for my relationships with all of you! To all the hands who have touched this book along the way, thank you!

Thank you to my parents for a childhood that encouraged curiosity and for teaching me not to give up but to finish what I start. God took those lessons and continues to teach me what it looks like to pursue Him. To Buds and Peytie, I love you both and am grateful to have family members who turned out to also be my friends.

Thank you to Tim and Chris Willard, who helped rekindle some of my own curiosity in Oxford, England, which led to an impromptu visit. Thanks to Blackwells bookstore, the Turf Tavern, and the random little nooks and crannies around town where I wrote and found pieces of myself again. Thanks to Biscuithead in Asheville for letting me cozy up in a corner by a bright window and write all day. To the Village Grind in Greenville, South Carolina, for making the most beautiful vanilla lavender latte ever and fueling many days for me.

I've always enjoyed reading this section of other books because it really does take a village to live a full life and work through a complete process. To the village that has surrounded me along the way … to teachers, mentors, friends, and family, written here and on my heart, thank you. I hope you enjoy reading this as much as I enjoyed writing it. It is my prayer that we all live curious … and rediscover the God of hope and possibility over and over again.

Notes

INTRODUCTION

1. C. S. Lewis, *The Weight of Glory and Other Addresses* (New York: Macmillan, 1980), 16.

CHAPTER 3

1. "No Ragrets," in *We're the Millers*, directed by Rawson Marshall Thurber (New Line Cinema, 2013).

CHAPTER 4

1. *Willy Wonka and the Chocolate Factory*, directed by Mel Stuart (Wolper Pictures, 1971).
2. Google search, s.v. "control," accessed September 29, 2015, www.google.com/webhp?sourceid=chrome-instant&rlz=1C1OPRA_enUS595US595&ion=1&espv=2&ie=UTF-8#q=define+control.
3. Robert Frost, "The Road Not Taken," in *Mountain Interval* (New York: Henry Holt, 1920).

CHAPTER 6

1. Robert Jamieson, A. R. Fausset, and David Brown, *Commentary Critical and Explanatory on the Whole Bible*, vol. 1 (Oak Harbor, WA: Logos Research Systems, 1997), 522.

CHAPTER 7

1. Father Daniel Homan, OSB, and Lonni Collins Pratt, *Radical Hospitality* (Brewster, MA: Paraclete, 2002), xxiv–xxv.

CHAPTER 9

1. Matthew Henry, *Matthew Henry's Commentary on the Whole Bible* (Peabody, MA: Hendrickson, 1994), 1755.
2. Thomas O. Chisholm, "Great Is Thy Faithfulness," © 1923 Hope Publishing.

CHAPTER 10

1. Bob Sorge, *Secrets of the Secret Place: Keys to Igniting Your Personal Time with God* (Grandview, MO: Oasis House, 2001), 24.

CHAPTER 11

1. Annie Dillard, *The Writing Life* (New York: Harper Perennial, 1990), 30.

CHAPTER 12

1. C. S. Lewis, *Mere Christianity* (San Francisco: HarperSanFrancisco, 1980), 226–27.

CHAPTER 13

1. Bob Sorge, *Secrets of the Secret Place: Keys to Igniting Your Personal Time with God* (Grandview, MO: Oasis House, 2001), 32.
2. C. S. Lewis, *The Lion, the Witch and the Wardrobe* (New York: Collier Books, 1970), 75–76.

Study Guide

INTRODUCTION

So, here's the deal, if you want to develop a more curious faith, it's gonna take a little effort to clear away some roadblocks, faith inhibitors if you will. Things like disappointments, lies about God, and various things that control you stand in the way of greater hope and curiosity. It's my desire that this study guide will help you do just that, clear the way. The idea is that I've included a range of questions and activities you can use to rediscover a more curious faith and hope in the God who does the unimaginable. The activities are arranged so that you can select those that are most helpful to you and leave the rest. For real, no pressure at all. If you want to dig deeper, great. If not, don't. I simply want to give you tools if you're in a season that you want them. You can also use the study guide with a group of friends whether you have just a few minutes or a couple of hours together. I've created it such that you can use the guide with or without the DVD series where I share about each topic in more depth. I pray that as you use this study guide, the

Bible passages and projects will lead you deep into the heart of the God who made the universe, covers the moon, and calls you His favorite. I want to help you become more curious and truly rediscover hope in the God of possibility.

INSTRUCTIONS

I have arranged the thirteen chapters of the book into an eight-week study, which in my experience is a sweet spot length of time for book studies and groups. While you can use it on your own, writing answers to the questions in a journal, I think you'll get more out of it if you grab some friends and do it in community. Agree on a day, a time, and a place to gather, and commit to meeting together for eight weeks to process what you're learning from the book.

Before you meet each week, read the assigned chapters and work through the Bible passage and the two projects. Have someone photocopy and cut out the "Talk About It" conversation cards, or download the prettier version from my website to use!

When you meet, plan to spend some time discussing the Bible passage and the projects. Then go through as many of the conversation cards as you have time for. If your time is limited, the group can choose which two or three of the cards are your top priorities for discussion. Have fun with it, and be willing to be honest and vulnerable.

GROUND RULES FOR GROUP DISCUSSION

If you want this to go well in a group, there are a handful of things that I think will not only help create a safe space, but also give permission for authentic and even vulnerable discussion. Some of them seem intuitive, but I think bear worth mentioning just to honor one another well:

- *Confidentiality:* Whatever is said in the group stays in the group. Nothing is to be repeated to those who weren't there. Honor one another by being trustworthy and protecting one another with confidentiality.

- *Honesty:* You're not here to impress one another. You're here to grow and to know one another. I was honest with you in these pages and want to encourage you that the best growth comes out of honest places of reflection.

- *Respect:* Play nice. It's totally fine to disagree, just make sure that in doing so, you don't disrespect another person. Jesus Himself was a gentleman even when addressing opposing views, so make sure that you are kind and respectful even if you find yourself on opposite sides of a discussion.

- *Conciseness:* As you share your answers to the questions, be conscious of allowing time for others to share. Don't be afraid to say what's on your mind, but don't ramble on for ages. Duh. The more people who can share, the more I believe you can grow and be challenged in new ways.

- *No Advice:* The idea here is to dig deeper into relationship with the Lord, not to solve one another's problems. Avoid trying to solve a group member's specific issues. For sure listen and care, but don't allow the discussion to become about giving advice. Just be cognizant to keep the discussion on track. Sometimes studies like this can open up cans of worms people didn't even realize they had in their lives. If that happens, encourage one another to seek professional help through a good counselor. It's the beauty of the body of Christ to encourage one another toward wholeness, and there is NO SHAME in needing some wise outside counsel!

Week 1
Read chapters 1 and 2

I hoped for a baby but ended up walking through a miscarriage. It was a devastating disappointment that rocked my entire faith.

I asked God for a church community but found myself leaving one in order to stay connected to Him in a healthy way. Talk about serious heartbreak in that too.

Why did God allow this pain and disappointment? Do you ever wonder that too? I mean, if God can cover the moon, if He is all-powerful, why does He allow suffering? It's the age-old question of "Why do bad things happen?"

When we struggle with questions like these, it's so tempting to put God in a box. Maybe He isn't really all-powerful. Maybe He isn't in charge at all times. Maybe God is no more impactful than your average social do-gooder.

This week, you read about disappointments and hitting rock bottom in your relationship with God. From there, you'll be challenged to start thinking about how hope is possible. I pray that as you spend time in God's presence with the Scriptures and the questions, the Lord will give you whole new vision of how big and good He is.

STUDY—READ ROMANS 8:31–39

How does this passage portray God?

God is …

God will …

God won't …

God …

God …

God …

When have you felt separated from the love of God?

What does this passage ask you to believe about that experience?

PROJECT 1

Ask yourself, "When I think of God, what do I see?" The answer to this question will help you see how you so easily box up God. He becomes limited by the experiences you have had and by the pictures in your imagination. It can be difficult to change a picture in your mind at first, but you can expand that picture so that it more closely resembles the God who really exists.

In your journal, list some character attributes of God that you have experienced in your life. Write some notes about the experiences.

Attribute	My Experience
Beauty	The music in my church growing up
Justice	Consequences for wrecking a car at age 16

What are some circumstances when God exceeded your expectations? How did He surprise you?

PROJECT 2

Unfortunately, life doesn't always exceed our expectations. It often lets us down. And disappointments can prevent us from trusting in God's character and believing in Him for big things, or even small things for that matter. These are what create the walls of the box we put around God. So right now, think of some of the biggest things you've asked God for in the past. Write down maybe two or three.

What happened? What was the outcome of those events or desires?

Think about the events or desires when you didn't get what you hoped for. What about those experiences made you feel most disappointed? What in you felt hurt most in the end?

Now think if there is anything at all good that may have come from those hard places. Did those things draw you closer or push you further from God? Have you learned any lessons?

What are you afraid to ask God for now?

TALK ABOUT IT

How have your disappointments shaped your present beliefs about God?	How has God brought redemption to you in the past?
How might God bring redemption to your current disappointments and struggles?	Is your view of God more colored by disappointment or hope? How?
What are you curious to know about God?	Where is rock bottom for you? What would it look like? Do you believe that God could redeem even that place? (This is a scary question to discuss, so give yourself and one another a lot of grace on this one.)

Week 2
Read chapter 3

Do you ever feel like there is an imaginary radio station in your head broadcasting nasty stuff about you? It doesn't really help plug your ears or try to sing another song louder to drown it out either. So rather than simply trying to ignore the lies, the challenge is to turn up the volume and really hear what is being said. Sometimes in order to speak the truth, we need to be able to name the lies we're believing first. We have to hear the ugly propaganda for what it is and then retune the channel of our minds to what is being said by the voice of God. Are you tracking with me? Hear the lies, but take them captive with the words of the Lord! What do ya say we give it a try?

STUDY—READ EPHESIANS 1:3–14

Make a list of the things Paul says are true of you in this passage.

Feel like having an argument with God? Write down all the reasons you don't entirely believe what Paul just said. "This can't be true because …" Pull out all the stops. What does your inner critic say when it hears all that great stuff about you?

This can't be true because …

Now write what God says back to you. Force yourself to go over-board here too!

> But God, being rich in mercy, because of the great love with which he loved us, even when we were dead in our trespasses, made us alive together with Christ … and raised us up with him and seated us with him in the heavenly places in Christ Jesus, so that in the coming ages he might show the immeasurable riches of his grace in kindness toward us in Christ Jesus. (Eph. 2:4–7)

Who are you really? Paul said God had great love for you even when you were dead in your sins. He said God made you alive together with Christ and reminds you that you are seated with Christ in the heavenly places. He did this so He could shower you with kindness. You are alive. You are seated in heavenly places. You are covered with the riches of God's grace. Chew on that for a minute my friend.

PROJECT 1

If you want to really develop a curious faith, then grab onto the truth of who God says you are by "praying the opposites." We have already run through this in chapter 3, but in case you kept reading and didn't try it yourself, here's your chance. This one exercise has honestly changed SO MUCH about the way I relate to God and see Him relate to me. If you do no other exercise in this book, do this one.

Step 1. Identify how you feel. "I feel confused, overwhelmed, guilty, ashamed, ecstatic, sad, lonely, hopeful, depressed, furious, frustrated, anxious, bored …"

Step 2. Name the lies about yourself. Give it a word or two. Think of the ugly words, the fruitless icky stuff.

Step 3. Now play the "opposite" game. Think of the complete opposites of your icky words. Use an antonym finder if you have to.

Step 4. Now that you have a list of encouraging words (the opposites of your icky ones), fruit of the Spirit even, look up Scripture passages that contain those words. You can search for your key words on Biblegateway.com or use a topical Bible like Openbible.info/topics/. Write down at least two relevant verses in your journal. I'll bet you will find even more than that though!

Step 5. Write your verses on Post-it notes. Put them on your mirror, your cabinets, anywhere you will see them regularly. Memorize these words that remind you of who you are.

Step 6. Put maybe one-tenth of your prayer time toward asking the Lord to get rid of your first list of icky words. The enemy would love nothing more than to have you camp out on his messy work … but you are the redeemed in Christ and have better things to do! Name it and move on! The point is, don't get hung up on your junk.

Step 7. Get down to business asking the Lord for all those lovely, positive, fruit-ridden words from your "opposite" list. Proclaim those benefits of heaven over your life, and believe the truth about who God says you are!

Step 8. Still feeling icky? Rinse and repeat until you've achieved a fresher you.

PROJECT 2

In your journal, draw a picture of how it feels to be broken free of those lies and living in the fruit-bearing truth of who God made you to be. Draw something even if you can do only stick figures and swirls. Write words that speak truth over you. Give yourself time to color or paint. It's not possible to mess this up! Allow our Creator to open a creative place in your spirit to consider His truth over you!

TALK ABOUT IT

Who are you right now? What do you believe about yourself?	What's the worst lie you have ever believed? What's the opposite of that lie?
What are the privileges of a daughter of the King?	If you fully embraced who you are, what are you afraid might be expected of you?
Read 2 Corinthians 5:17. How are you a new creation?	What is God calling you toward?

Week 3
Read chapters 4 and 5

Do you know why people who are afraid to fly in an airplane will calmly start the engine of a car and drive away? Despite statistical evidence saying one is more likely to die in a car accident than a plane crash, when we drive a car we feel in control. In a plane, we believe our fate lies in the hands of another outside of our influence. The illusion of control is what keeps us feeling confident. Never mind that we have no impact over what other drivers do.

More often than I want to admit, I'm totally that person. Control so often makes me feel safe as if I have the power to order outcomes. But what I need most really is to trust God enough to let go of control.

STUDY—READ EXODUS 14:5-14

God afflicted Egypt with plagues until Pharaoh couldn't stand it anymore and finally let the Israelite slaves leave the country and set off into the wilderness. What did Pharaoh do next?

How did the Israelites respond? Why? What was it like for them to not be in control?

Read Exodus 14:15–30. How did God handle the situation?

Do you believe that God would come through for you like that? What helps you believe it? What gets in the way?

What if the situation was messier and God took longer to bring you through a trial? What would you do?

PROJECT 1

Write down some of the ways you try to control life around you. How does that control manifest itself?

What does your effort to control things prevent you from experiencing?

My minivan seemed to ridicule me for having only one child when I'd planned for more. Is there something specific you feel mocks you and keeps you from experiencing the goodness of God?

From your list, choose maybe one area of control that you want to specifically release, and spend some time working on how you can change that. Apply the following Scripture passages to that situation. Rephrase each passage in a way that applies to you personally. You can put your name into the passage or restate the passage in your own words. If these passages aren't doing it for you today, dig in deeper and look up some more of your own.

> He who dwells in the shelter of the Most High
> will abide in the shadow of the Almighty.
> I will say to the LORD, "My refuge and my
> fortress,
> my God, in whom I trust."

For he will deliver you from the snare of the
    fowler
    and from the deadly pestilence.
He will cover you with his pinions,
    and under his wings you will find refuge;
    his faithfulness is a shield and buckler.
        (Ps. 91:1–4)

No temptation has overtaken you that is not common to man. God is faithful, and he will not let you be tempted beyond your ability, but with the temptation he will also provide the way of escape, that you may be able to endure it. (1 Cor. 10:13)

God is our refuge and strength,
    a very present help in trouble.
Therefore we will not fear though the earth
    gives way,
    though the mountains be moved into the
    heart of the sea,
though its waters roar and foam,
    though the mountains tremble at its
    swelling. (Ps. 46:1–3)

PROJECT 2

Are you in a wilderness or a hallway of possibility? What got you here? Write down the things in your life that leave you feeling lonely, forgotten, disappointed, or angry. If you think possibility is before you, list some of those out as well.

What are you longing for that hasn't come to pass? Make a list in your journal. Beside your list, write the way it makes you feel. Do you feel sad? Do you feel forgotten? Expectations unmet? Perhaps you're just angry how things haven't gone the way you hoped. Give yourself space to really bring these things before the Lord. He isn't afraid of your honesty, so go there with Him. Tell Him how you're really feeling. Give yourself permission to be completely honest before God.

What I'm longing for	How I feel

So what are you going to do about it?

Begin to consider some of the blessings in your life. Write down a handful of things you're thankful for.

Search the Scriptures for the blessing that God has for you. (Hello, online concordance!) Search for the words in Scripture that you're looking for and see what God says about them.

Record your hopes and dreams that have come to pass. Testimony is the remembering of what God has done already. Shore up your faith by remembering the goodness that you have already experienced.

PROJECT 3

Identify someone you know whose life seems to go exactly the way she wants. Call her or make a coffee date and ask her secrets. Find out if the perceived perfection is really true. How does she manage it? (Please email me her name later. I want to be friends too! But for real, let's be honest, no matter how perfect you think someone else's life may be … we all have struggles.)

TALK ABOUT IT

What is some good that has come from your pain?	What is one of your expectations? What happens if it doesn't get met?
What are you trying so hard to control that it has robbed you of a capacity to make your way toward a new promise?	Imagine that all your dreams did come true. What would be the hard parts of those new things?
What are some of the possible doors that you might need to try opening?	How could God use this wilderness experience in your life?

Week 4
Read chapters 6 and 7

When I'm in a mind-set of control rather than curiosity, the thing I most want to control is the future. Because I can't control it, I'm tempted to worry about it. Never mind that worry never added a minute to anybody's life span or deducted a minute of pain. Somehow, imagining the things that could happen feels like a way to control the outcome.

Waiting patiently for the future instead of worrying about it or getting impatient for it to come takes practice. Slow, gradual practice—day by day and hour by hour. I choose each hour to be curious about the future instead of stressing about it. "What's next, Lord?" I pray with an expectant smile and unclenched hands. "What do You have for me now?"

STUDY—READ ISAIAH 35:3–7

What reason for not being anxious does Isaiah give here?

What picture of the future does this passage give?

What kind of God can promise a future like this?

Take a moment to let yourself imagine this scenario playing out. It actually happened during Jesus's earthly ministry, so it's not some way-out impossible future. Picture the scene, and let yourself rest in it. You might even draw one of the images from the scene. How does God want this to be true in your life?

PROJECT 1

I learned something in counseling a few years ago that helps me battle my tendency to worry. They told me to imagine Jesus with me in my past scenarios that continue to bug me, and also to imagine Him even in the future scenarios I'm fabricating and worrying about. Since God says He will never leave me, I know that Jesus is always there.

I'm super right brained, so it helps me to almost daydream about a situation and invite Jesus into it. He is always there. Most of the time He's even holding my hand. That's how He is.

Try this idea yourself. It can be a real encouragement just to remember that no matter what scenario you dream up in your active imagination, Jesus is there. For crying out loud, though, don't just let yourself cook up all sorts of ridiculous scenarios. And when you imagine Jesus in them, make sure you're only applying attributes to Him that you see in Scripture (kindness, understanding, love, etc.). Don't let the enemy get a foothold in your imagination. Hold on to truth.

PROJECT 2

Pray the opposites about something that is worrying you. Or something you're waiting for. I'm telling you … this method can be your ticket to so much freedom!

Step 1. Identify how you feel. "I feel worried, anxious, impatient, frustrated ..."

Step 2. Name the thing you're afraid will happen.

Step 3. Now play the "opposite" game. Think of the complete opposite of worry, anxiety, or whatever you're feeling or fearing.

Step 4. Look up Scripture passages that contain those words. For instance, you can look for passages about confidence, rest, trust, God's faithfulness, or God's goodness. Or just start reading through Isaiah 40–43 and write down relevant promises you find there.

Step 5. Write your verses on Post-it notes. Put them on your mirror, your cabinets, anywhere you will see them regularly. Memorize these words that remind you of what is true.

Step 6. Pray your chosen verses over your situation.

PROJECT 3

Every night for the next week before you go to sleep, write down three things that went well today. Studies have shown that six months afterward, people felt overall more pleased with their lives. And when you're feeling positive, you're less likely to give yourself over to worry.

TALK ABOUT IT

Write down some things you are thankful for.	What's the best thing you think could happen to you?
Is God big enough to overcome your fears? How do you know?	What are you waiting for right now?
How long are you willing to wait? Why that timetable?	What can you do now that you won't be able to do when this season shifts?

Week 5
Read chapters 8 and 9

Rather than allowing life's fluctuating circumstances to define our stability, we will find greater security and contentment when we allow the truth of Christ to be the defining factor. We learn to manage the tensions of life without freezing up. We look back at the past with appreciation and gratitude without a nostalgia that makes us dissatisfied in the present. A centeredness in Christ will allow us to look forward to the future while making real decisions for the here and now.

Are you so afraid you settled in the past that you have stopped living curiously for your future? Or are you so afraid of settling into the wrong thing that you never actually land on anything at all? Are you living your life looking backward, or looking so far forward at so many options that you have analysis-paralysis and can't make a decision at all? Let's make some decisions today.

STUDY—READ MARK 1:14–39

Jesus began his ministry in the shadow of his cousin John's arrest for his own ministry (v. 14). How did that threat color Jesus's own actions? Did it seem to affect Jesus's choices? How or how not?

How did Jesus decide what moves to make (vv. 35–39)?

Evaluate Jesus's early ministry for signs of wanderlust, indecisiveness, or settling for good enough. What do you observe?

It didn't take long for the tension to rise in Jesus's ministry. Read Mark 3:1–6. Why didn't Jesus avoid what He knew would make dangerous enemies?

How would you like to imitate Jesus in the way He dealt with life?

PROJECT 1

In your journal, write down some of what you've been looking at in your past and comparing to your present.

What about that past thing do you think was so much better? What in that scenario do you think was more promising or life giving? Ask yourself, and make yourself answer. Why do you think that?

Now, sister … let it go. Have a cry, and let it go. Your past is not your future.

PROJECT 2

Maybe you're Wendy Wanderlust and are still "better-dealing" your whole life. Write down the glorious future that you're imagining for yourself. Make a list of all you're waiting for in order to live inside of those dreams. Be descriptive and thorough. This is, after all, your perfect scenario.

Can we have a moment here and ask how much of that is realistic? Let's recognize that no relationship will be without issues, no job will be without stresses, no responsibility without responsibility. If you get a dog, it will need walking. It will love you, but it might poop in your house. If you get a house for your dog to poop in, you will love the season of ownership. You will love having something to call you own. But pipes will burst and cost a ton of money during a hard freeze.

What are you afraid of? What are you afraid you're going to miss? I want you to search the Scriptures for all of the promises of God for His children. And I'll tell you a spoiler alert here too: you're never going to miss out on anything that God has for your life when you follow Him.

PROJECT 3

Remember the click-clack rhythm of Newton's Cradle? One hanging ball goes *click*, and the one on the far end goes *clack*.

Let's consider some of the click-clacks of life. Write down a few of the swings you've experienced this week, month, or year.

Draw a time line in your journal. Today should be at the far right end, and the past works backward from there. Refer to the example below, but feel free to change the scale to a week or a month instead of a year.

12	11	10	9	8	7	6	5	4	3	2	1
Months ago											Today

Plot out your upswings above the line and your downswings below the line. I bet you can begin to see how life swings back and forth between moments and even seasons.

As you look at the swings, write where you are finding your joy. Is your joy in your circumstances alone, or are you able to look through the lens of Christ to still see His goodness?

What helps you look through the filter of Christ? Write down scriptures, people, and activities that have encouraged you in times of need. The next time you're finding yourself on a downswing, pull out these reminders as testimony of what the Lord has already done for you. And in the upswings, go back to your reminders to fortify your faith even more.

TALK ABOUT IT

What do you need to trust God for right now?	What are you waiting for?
What is some goodness of this season?	What do you need to release?
What are you settling for?	What do you think is God's best for you now?

Week 6
Read chapter 10

When something in your life has broken, it takes time to heal. Just like breaking a limb, there needs to be a period of setting and renewing to return to wholeness. But unlike broken bones, life doesn't always return to the exact state it was in before. It will be new and redeemed one day because of the goodness of God, but life won't ever be as if the thing that broke you never happened.

To find healing in your most raw and broken places, you first have to expose them. But don't just expose them to yourself when you begin to write them down, expose them to Jesus. He is enough. He may not feel like enough yet, and it may take a long time for your heart to be satisfied with Him. But that's where you're headed: to a place where your soul begins to hope and know that Jesus is enough for you.

STUDY—READ MATTHEW 27:27–50

Imagine yourself as a participant in this scene. Stand among the soldiers, follow the procession to Golgotha, and stand with the crowd at the cross. What do you see at each point? What do you hear? What smells and physical sensations are you aware of? What do you feel? What do you want to say to the other participants or to Jesus? What do you do? Take some time with this. Let the events play out like a movie, frame by frame, and pay attention to what's going on with the various characters as it happens.

Think about your own experience of trauma or loss or heaviness in the context of this scene. What are the hard things, the raw things, the wrong things, the unfair things that cripple your faith and break your heart? Can you see Jesus carrying your experience? Give it to Him in some way: hand it over physically, or tell Him about it as the scene is playing out. What does He do with it? How does His response affect you?

Spend some time journaling to the Lord the things you are thinking as you do this exercise. Work out your faith and frustrations armed with the truth of God's love and sacrifice for you.

PROJECT 1

What is a current heavy struggle that you're facing? Or what is an ongoing struggle where you have yet to see redemption?

What would redemption look like to you? How would it play out in your life?

How can you best manage this struggle if you never see the redemption?

Do you think you'll be okay? Why or why not?

Laying things at the cross once won't necessarily magically make everything better permanently. If your heavy burden is a significant loss or pain, you'll probably have to give it to Jesus over and over as you discover new parts of yourself feeling broken from the same things. In this place, there is no good answer but the cross. There is no reconciliation besides Jesus Himself before you. I want to encourage you to stop trying to make sense of the senseless. Stop trying to find ways to explain the broken, and instead start finding ways to walk yourself through it. Wrestle for the blessing that is promised to you in Jesus.

PROJECT 2

Make a coffee or lunch date with someone to talk about the struggle you're in and the release you're longing for. Cling to hope, and walk curiously after the sweet God of restoration.

Writing this book, I wrote and prayed this prayer over you. Pray it for yourself, claim the life and hope that are for you in Christ:

Sweet Jesus, we speak Your peaceful presence over the broken places of our lives right now. Lord, we lay down the irreconcilable in this world before You and ask that You fill our spirits up with Your heavenly reconciliation. Father God, we ask that You would breathe life into dry bones, that You would expose hope in dark places, and that You would pour out blessing over our weary souls. Jesus, You are the redemption of our brokenness, and we thank You that in You, and You alone, we can find peace and rest. Amen.

TALK ABOUT IT

What are you wrestling with God about?	What will it look like to wrestle well?
What blessing can come from your wrestle?	Have you taken your anger to God? What happened?
Are you allowing your brokenness to define you? How?	How are you being redeemed from your brokenness?
Is Jesus enough for you? Why or why not?	If not, what would be enough for you?

Week 7
Read chapters 11 and 12

So often it feels as if life conspires to keep us from moving forward. There will always be laundry and dishes and a hundred other tasks that need to be done just for survival, just to keep a roof over our heads and food in our mouths. But still the Lord calls our names, asking us to say yes in tiny ways to the workings of His kingdom.

Curiosity is what moves us to raise our heads over the pile of laundry and say, "What's that You're saying, Lord? I'm here. I'm listening. Where are You leading me?" Then we take a step, maybe not with total confidence but with curiosity to find out where the path will take us.

STUDY—READ MATTHEW 21:28–32

What point was Jesus making in this parable?

How were the tax collectors and prostitutes of Jesus's day like the first son?

Right now, do you identify more with the first son or the second? Why?

PROJECT 1

In your journal, draw or describe yourself on the path God currently has you facing. Maybe the way is clearly marked out with brightly colored arrows. Maybe it's wreathed in fog. Maybe you're looking at a choice between three possible roads. The path may be smooth or rocky, steeply uphill or winding down and down. It could be dark except for the light illumining your next step forward.

PROJECT 2

Think of an area of your life where you can say a tiny yes to God. Is there an idea you've had that piques your curiosity? Have you been asked to participate in something but maybe you have been too nervous to do it? Is there something you started and quit that perhaps you need to pick back up again?

Write down a few of the reasons that you resist saying yes. Now consider if your reasons line up with Scripture or if they are rooted in fear. If it's fear or worry, then I want to encourage you to maybe even hop back to Week 4 and go through one of those projects to address fear and worry again.

Because I believe testimony is a powerful tool for remembering God's faithfulness to us, think of a few times when you said yes to something that turned out to be a crossroads or to present an entirely new opportunity for you.

PROJECT 3

Maybe, like me, your life seems to get jam-packed and you don't have enough room for variation. What are some ways you can create space for yourself? Don't fall victim to the lie that creating some time for you is selfish. A whole you is one that is cared for. What are things, people, or situations that feel life giving to you? Write down a few of those things, and then set some goals to make time for you to do them.

And here's the really crazy part: get out your calendar and make that space. Put it down, and don't delete it!

TALK ABOUT IT

What step could really go somewhere if you gave it time, space, and consistency?	What small things can you change to shift your perspective?
How could you create space for some self-care?	How could you create space for your spouse to do some self-care?
What keeps you stuck in the same patterns?	List some ways you get off of your familiar path and try something new.

Week 8
Read chapter 13

What legacy do you want to leave to your children and others around you? A curious faith lives in hope, running forward toward an infinite God who defies possibility. It impacts your life even now because it is defined by the goodness of the God who offers hope for the future.

What do you want people to remember about the way you engage with your life? What qualities of faith do you want to pass on? Are you ready to let go? Do you believe that God is for you and that he has hope and possibility for your life? Are you ready to jump into your life, aware of what's around, allowing the unknown not to paralyze, but to catalyze you into a fuller life?

Thank you for launching out on this path. You're not alone. I pray that God will multiply your investment so that your legacy is brighter and longer than you can possibly imagine.

STUDY—READ NUMBERS 13:17–14:9

Moses sent twelve men to spy out the land of Canaan before the Israelites went in to claim it as their Promised Land. Ten of the spies brought back a discouraging report; two (Caleb and Joshua) had a different view. What were the positive things about the Promised Land (13:23, 27)?

What were the dangers (13:28–29, 32–33)?

What arguments did Joshua and Caleb offer for not giving in to fear (13:30; 14:6–9)?

How does this story speak to your situation?

PROJECT 1

What is something that God has stirred in you throughout this book that you are curious to uncover with Him? What will it look like to jump in?

Think back on a couple of areas where you have felt most challenged throughout the book. How do you plan to keep moving forward? What do you most want to take with you from this journey?

PROJECT 2

Write a prayer to God about the legacy you want to leave to those who come after you and the situation you are facing now. Be brutally honest about how you're feeling, and don't hesitate to dream big.

Now write what you think God could be saying in response to your prayer.

TALK ABOUT IT

What do you want others to gain from your life?	What kind of legacy do you hope you leave when you're gone?
How have you seen God's goodness?	Who might not want you to take this next step?
Who will encourage you as you move forward?	What is the unknown that's hard to face?
What do you dare to hope for?	